Y0-BGG-427

Since Stephen

A Parent's Examination of Reality

Since Stephen

A Parent's Examination of Reality

Catherine Poelman

Illustrated by Marc Boyden

Northwest Publishing, Inc.
Salt Lake City, Utah

Since Stephen

All rights reserved.
Copyright © 1995 Northwest Publishing, Inc.

Reproduction in any manner, in whole or in part,
in English or in other languages, or otherwise
without written permission of the publisher is prohibited.

For information address: Northwest Publishing, Inc.
6906 South 300 West, Salt Lake City, Utah 84047
JC 2.9.95

PRINTING HISTORY
First Printing 1995

ISBN: 1-56901-438-8

NPI books are published by Northwest Publishing, Incorporated,
6906 South 300 West, Salt Lake City, Utah 84047.
The name "NPI" and the "NPI" logo are trademarks belonging to
Northwest Publishing, Incorporated.

PRINTED IN THE UNITED STATES OF AMERICA.
10 9 8 7 6 5 4 3 2 1 .

For my husband and children
as we adjust to the death of our son and brother
who took his life
after twenty eventful years.

Preface

My dream was to raise all of our children to be responsible adults. My son, Stephen, died May 11, 1991. He jumped off a parking plaza. As the dream perished, I was left to hope for some good from this tragedy.

Five months later I found Stephen's writings in a sack. I began a search to evaluate myself as a parent. Stephen's honesty quickened my own. Through his eyes I examined our common ground.

What flowed were stark, embarrassing experiences in my past; they stood out awkwardly above the natural current of life. At first I believed they were worthless to others, but they showed me purpose in it all. Without my mistakes I was not real. I studied them and marveled that my personal errors did not hurt like tragedy. I could work with them. I began to lose my fear; in the process of mending I was improving.

My dream revised. Stephen was one of life's casualties. He did not die as I had dreaded. He never crashed on his motorcycle or slipped from the Mill roof but he broke down inside. I learned from him. I continue to hope.

—Catherine Poelman

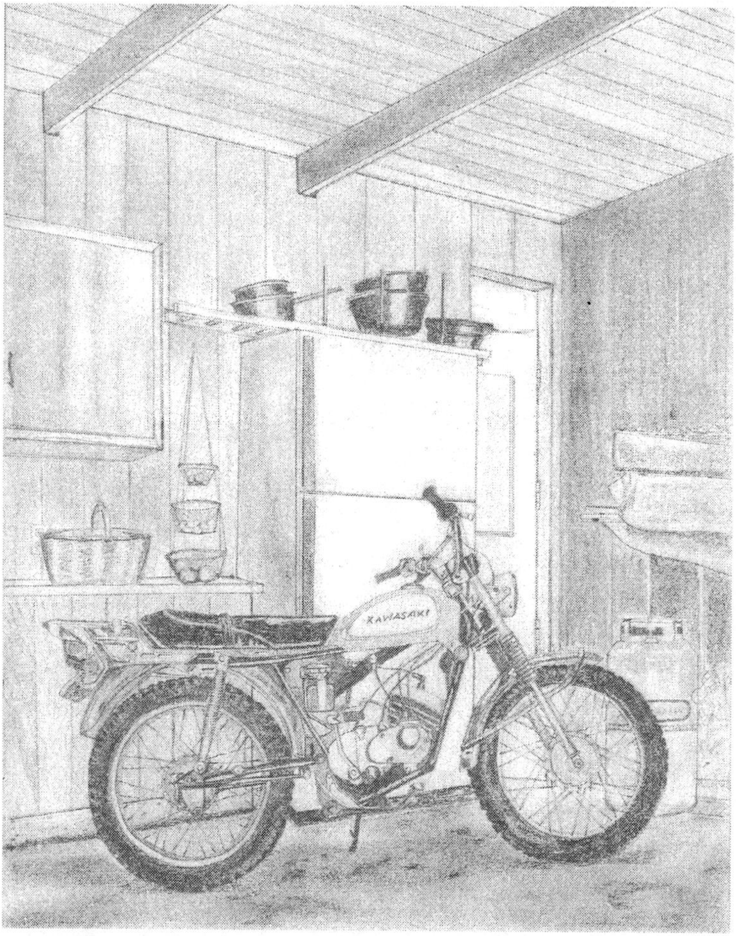
KAWASAKI

one

Since Stephen

"They topple grave stones, Mom," Martha said, watching a chicken patty rotate inside the microwave oven. She was telling me about other teenagers she heard talking at the high school. "That's what they do for fun at night." We were standing together in the nearly finished kitchen of our old Mill where we always go when school is out. Martha, our seventh child, is four years younger than Stephen.

"Dang it, that's awful," I said. "They don't know anything!"

"Think of the people, Mom."

"I'm thinking of their families."

"That's what I mean."

1

Stephen's grave, so fresh it had no tombstone, roused in me new anger against reckless teenagers, until I remembered my son had been one.

After tearing lettuce into a salad bowl for a few minutes, I calmed down. Martha had remained quiet, fixing her no-fat chicken burger. She sat down to eat on the motorcycle parked inside the Mill's back door.

"Did problems begin with our example?" I asked her. "Was it wrong for us to enjoy riding?"

"It had nothing to do with example, Mom. Motorcycles are fun."

Our 90cc Kawasaki is over twenty years old. We keep it at the Mill—our family retreat—so my husband, Lloyd, and I can ride the quiet canyon road to Blue Pond Spring, with nature coming at us, breezing around us. I like adventure and motorcycles but I'm vulnerable now, compelled to evaluate myself, examining everything in my life since Stephen died.

The year Stephen was born we took a get-away trip from our home in Salt Lake City, to Las Vegas. Lloyd and I rented a motorcycle to go to Lake Mead.

"Do you know how to ride?" the owner asked.

"I'm sure we'll manage." Outside the shop I waited while Lloyd practiced driving around the parking lot a couple of times.

Gangs of motorcyclists passed us as we rode on Highway 146, exposed and intimate amongst red rock masses. They waved in their studded leather jackets. We didn't know anyone in Nevada. We waved back.

A few months later Lloyd bought a used Kawasaki motorcycle. After our four girls were in bed one evening, he surprised me with two helmets.

"Let's go riding."

"I'm pregnant."

"Just a quick ride through the canyon. We won't go over any bumps."

We started in the warm air near the Capitol, curving down through City Creek Canyon, and then climbing up to the north bench leveling off on the road above the cemetery where we stopped to view the city lights down in the valley.

"How do you like the motorcycle? It's not dangerous is it?" he asked.

On the way back I put one arm around Lloyd and one hand under me to cushion any impact from dips in the road. Motorcycle rides became a summer night habit. Daily concerns vanished in the darkness as the wind whipped by our faces and flapped our clothes. We wore helmets as much for disguise as protection.

While on a trip to the South Seas for a conference, Lloyd and I had six free hours in Tahiti before meetings began in the evening. We walked the streets of Papeete past modern businesses, noisy traffic and hundreds of beeping cycles. Wandering back into dirt streets where children played ball between banana trees and sleeping animals, we saw the volcanic mountain ranges towering in front of us. We felt trapped in the city until we found a cycle rental shop.

On a motorcycle we rode up the coast highway, looking down from black cliffs to palms and blue water. Jutting out was a hotel flanked by pools and tiers of patios covered with tables. We hid our motorcycle in foliage by the hotel vans. Walking along a path leading to the outdoor cafe, we recognized the leader who would preside over the conference and his wife. They joined us for a cold drink. We followed them back toward their room, turning out at the parking lot.

"Where are you going? Aren't you staying here? How did you come?" They insisted on watching us retrieve the motorcycle and waited laughing while we buckled our helmets, giving cheers as we left.

I was relieved to get back safely in the rush hour traffic. We had broken our cautious pattern of riding on quiet streets at off-hours and we treasured the adventure. As we returned to our hotel after the evening meetings, we watched a wrecked motorcycle being hauled away.

"Accidents are very common here," the hotel clerk said. "Motorcycles are so dangerous, you know."

We moved to Tennessee for three years before any of our children were old enough to drive, so we stored the motorcycle in my brother's garage. "We must get rid of the Kawasaki before the children want to use it," I said. Lloyd agreed.

We didn't use the motorcycle the year we returned to Utah. The younger children got rides on a new Suzuki 125 owned by our daughter's boyfriend. He was a football hero at the high school; he loved children. Stephen, Mike and Martha would line up in the driveway for their turn and often load the two small boys, Andrew and John, on too. If there wasn't enough room on the seat, they rode on the gas tank or rear fender. Lloyd and I tried to ignore it. The young man was careful and the rides were only around a few blocks in our neighborhood.

"Let's teach motorcycle safety," I said to Lloyd, "since they're riding anyway." I proposed that we take the family to Canyonlands for spring break. We could carry the Kawasaki and a friend's three-wheeler in the van, traveling tandem with the old motorhome. The idea appealed to all ages—our oldest child was twenty and our youngest three.

In the late afternoon, we drove west out of Moab on Cane Creek Road for two miles and parked. While I started dinner, the first group went exploring. When I caught up, two children had gone further down the road on the three-wheeler, others were perched on a rock two hundred feet above the road, and Stephen sat on the motorcycle watching other boys far below in a gulch, twisting and jumping over mounds with their high powered dirt bikes.

"Can I go down a ways?" Stephen asked.

"You don't have the power or the traction they do. I wouldn't go far."

Lloyd and I took our youngest child and started on foot up the mountain. We stopped to rest and watched Stephen slide down dirt and sage to the gulch below. The old motorcycle created a handicap except as a pretext for watching the other boys up close.

I rode back to camp at twilight. Lloyd waited for Stephen to pull the bike up onto the road. He didn't need or want help. Stephen had cut the cable to the wheel drive on his Snapper lawn mower the year before so he could push manually and build muscles. He had a "company partner"; they worked fifteen lawn jobs together.

The next day Stephen scaled the canyon wall without the bike. The rest of us were wading and skipping rocks in a pond near camp. Lloyd watched him from a distance. Stephen was stuck in one place for twenty minutes with his hands on a ledge above him before he asked for help. Sound traveled around the gorge and made Stephen's voice audible to all of us, even though he was a hundred feet up at the other end of the ravine.

"Dad...I can't see how to get down."

Lloyd called out instructions. Everyone else was quiet and moved closer. Stephen's strength was giving out; he couldn't respond. It took time for Lloyd to climb up underneath him and get stable. Stephen had to use Lloyd's hand as a foothold to get off the first ledge.

When we were back together, the other children could see that it was easier to get up than down. Lloyd saw trust between him and his son. I saw Stephen's passion for adventure. Had I compared my youth to his, I could have understood. But I had changed. Interim years as a parent focused me on protecting my children. A gap had developed between us.

"Stephen's riding in the park," a youngster told me the year Stephen got his driver's license.

"You'd better go and see."

I ran down the street. Stephen was slowly driving over the sidewalk onto the grass which undulated for half a block past the playground equipment to a side street in his old Dasher. I ran to the passenger window.

"What are you doing?"

Stephen didn't look at me; I wasn't sure he heard my voice through the glass. He was riveted on the scene in front of him. It was dusk, no lights were on.

"Stephen!" I pounded on the window. Another car, which his friend was driving, crept over the grass toward us.

"I'm leaving, Mom," Stephen said. His voice was clear, his window had been open the whole time. He still didn't look at me. His friend circled a flowering plum tree in front of us and drove back onto the street with Stephen following.

While Stephen worked in Hawaii he wrote, "I like the crazy life 'cause you're scared and never know what's going to happen…like jumping extra high on a motorcycle, trying things that are dangerous. There's something about it that gives you energy—you do things out of fright you never thought you could do and probably couldn't do without being as scared as you are."

Months later Stephen bought a 200 XR dirt bike. "Don't worry, Mom. It's not even street legal. I'll have my fun in the mountains."

I was sitting behind Stephen in the hearing room when the traffic judge asked him how many tickets he had received since he got his license.

"I can't remember," he said. He wasn't being insolent. No one could get his attention yet.

When Stephen died, I searched minds I trusted. I knew I would read scriptures over again just like I knew I would reread the classics. On one of those days, Dostoyevsky described a young man like Stephen. He "rushed headlong on another path, to meet peril and danger, compelled to this course by nobody and by nothing, but as it were, simply disliking the beaten track."

In December when Stephen turned eighteen, he skipped school to ski and broke his collar bone jumping on the first run. He rebroke it three times, twice on his dirt bike before he sold it and once on the Aero 125 scooter he bought when he couldn't get insurance.

My imagination failed me. There was nothing I could say to Stephen that he hadn't heard. His love of adventure cut the primary ties to us and he darted away independent, unprotected by experience. He wasn't fighting me or Lloyd or a moral code anymore. He was fighting nature and law.

The unlicensed Aero 125 was impounded by the University after two warnings. The day Stephen bought a license and got it out of hock (for more money than he paid for it) the clutch gave out.

"Incredible, isn't it, Mom?" he said. "I can't believe what happens to me."

The scooter remained useless in the carport for the next two years until he died. Only when Stephen was no longer around to scare me with his wildness, could I see how much he enjoyed his reckless phase.

two

The Rural Life

The emergency call about Stephen came while we were at the Mill. Lloyd was getting a load of wood and when he returned I told him right there in our bedroom by the cupboards Stephen framed, that our son had jumped off a sixty foot parking plaza. I wondered if subsequent trips would be painful, but they are renewing. Stephen is built into the Mill like the rest of us.

To get to the Mill from our Utah home we drive for three hours northeast to a small farming community in Idaho near Bear Lake. The road sign says the population is 211. After passing the town market we turn west and can see it on the old highway. It was once a grist mill and saw mill; later a

Chevrolet dealership had been added. "1915" was drawn in the cement floor of what is now our kitchen.

The first time we saw the Mill was Labor Day weekend, 1985. All of our children were with us, except one older daughter studying in London. Lloyd and I had come to the same community earlier in the summer to stay overnight with friends who annually invited us. I had resisted the drive, the time away, and the pep talk about what a good project fixing up an old farm house had been for their family. But I had come and toured their places—they were working on a third house.

On Saturday morning our friend, still in his fishing boots, bent down in the charred parlor of his latest project to demonstrate how to strip wood. He brushed Strypeeze onto a turquoise baseboard and waited for a few seconds. Then, lying on the floor with scraper in hand, he cleaned the wrinkled paint off—exclaiming, gesturing, laughing at his progress as stream water leaked in puddles around his feet. For him menial labor was desirable.

I was transformed. Yes, I wanted a project to strengthen our family; I wanted to search for a place of our own that day. I looked over at Lloyd. He was watching politely, unmoved.

When we arrived home in the evening I told Stephen, then fourteen, and Mike, just a year younger, about my "old house fantasy," describing each abandoned structure I had seen on the way back. They fueled my idea.

"We've got to prove to Dad what we can do," Stephen said. We studied about chain saws and purchased one together so Stephen and Mike could trim the fifty foot elm trees in our yard at home. Mike and I held the ladder and stacked the limbs. Stephen climbed and cut. Am I courting danger? I wondered as I watched Stephen dangling above my head steadying the roaring blade. But I knew that without me, he would be doing something just as scary and not as constructive. The next week we wallpapered and painted the boys' bathroom. Lloyd had noticed.

"I'll go back up and look around for a day," he said in

August.

He reported, "There's a big old barn place for sale—just a shell filled with junk."

When we walked into the Mill as a family I was unprepared. The main floor was heaped with old machinery, box springs, pots, furniture. Wasp hives clung to the beams next to bird nests. The upstairs was better—less junk, but the roof and walls admitted daylight between every slat, except where cardboard had been tacked up. Connected to the wood section was a concrete side that looked unsafe; cement poured around wire between train rails had comprised the upper floor. Now, most of the cement had crumbled onto the first level. A keg of spilled tar covered one corner. We could peek up through the wire to ten cement grain bins on the second story. Two of them had funnels that emptied into rusty grinders. The dilapidated roof was caving in. For thirty-three years this partially rebuilt structure had stood abandoned.

"I 'spose you'll jest bulldoze down the cement part," the neighbor said. "Don't look worth nothin' to me." He watched the Mill for the three out-of-state men who owned their grandfather's estate. He left his two dogs outside and strolled around in the main room with hands in his pockets explaining about the three acres of land. The property went up the hill, past the old trucks and barn foundation to the fence, then through the woods and down to the swamp. He accompanied us downstairs with a flashlight to see the fresh water spring, containing rusty machine parts and a few small fish, which channeled through two underground storage rooms.

It was too much—too big, too run down, too demanding. And we wanted it; even Lloyd could see the advantage for our family. Stephen and Mike couldn't stop smiling. The near impossibility of the challenge triggered enthusiasm in everyone except our fourth daughter. "It's sick," she said. "I'll cook for others but I can't work."

Along with our meager purchase offer to the owners, Lloyd sent a letter describing our family's eagerness to work together. Lloyd's desire for the project had caught up, and then surpassed mine. The offer was accepted. The following summer a grandson of the original owner came from Nevada to see the progress in a cardigan sweater and slacks. Lloyd was up on the roof with Stephen and Mike. For three days they had been working together, stuffing themselves at D.J.'s Diner in the evenings. They had yanked the rotting boards off the concrete side and were pounding in a network of 2"x16" beams and metal plates. The visitor watched for an hour, seated on the center beam. He did not speak. Forty years ago this man had left a shop light running on a car seat. It started a fire that destroyed the Mill. Only the concrete skeleton had remained. His grandfather had been rebuilding the Mill himself until he died. He had spent his Social Security checks on nails and procured lumber from the Ovid mill on credit.

During our first autumn as owners, we loaded our new neighbor's dump truck twice, once with machinery and once with junk. We shoveled out the crumbled cement and put windows in the wood section. The weather stayed good while we nailed cedar siding on two exterior walls and put a coat of tar paper on the roof. Inside, a week before the first snow, we installed the wood burning stove on a brick base.

For two years, every weekend and every holiday we returned to the Mill to make it more livable. Our sons brought their friends; our daughter's boyfriends were tested for skills and character. Like Thoreau, we "wanted to live deep and suck out the marrow of life, to live so sturdily...as to put to rout all that was not life." We had Mill clothes which were stained, torn, and always with nails in the pockets.

One week in the summer I took the boys to the Mill with Martha. Lloyd couldn't go and he was nervous we'd ruin it. Stephen and Mike brought the friend who shared their passion for building, the "company partner."

"Plan what materials you need to cover the south wall with cupboards," I said to them in our future bedroom. They measured before we headed to the store in Montpelier, refiguring all the way into town. I stood back while they made sure the clerk selected the best wood. I gave no suggestions, even when they asked. I expected they knew more about carpentry from their shop class in school than I did.

The cupboards were framed in two days. We swam at the Hot Springs in the evenings and read by lantern light, *Death Be Not Proud*, the struggle of a young boy with cancer.

After they were asleep, I lay in the dark on one of six secondhand beds curtained off from the porta-potty area trying to understand what kept pulling us to the Mill. Rural labor appealed to our bodies and souls. The pioneers would have understood. So would Rousseau.

Other opinions ceased to matter—I was free. When guests looked in on us and tried to comprehend our focus, they pulled back from the unreasonableness they saw. I told them that the steel rails made the concrete side structurally sound and would be covered with pine planks, that the ten grain bins would make eight cozy bedrooms and two bathrooms, that next to the spring in the basement would be a root cellar and workshop safely enclosed by a trap door. I visualized the metamorphosis completed. I knew perseverance would take us there gradually, and they stood there being sorry for me.

"No wonder you got it for such a good price. Do you think you'll ever finish?" The process was the essence. I had teenage children who followed me away from crowds to isolation. My father understood. "It would be better if you never finished," he said.

I wanted to be tethered to nature; beauty sprawled out in the country. My fantasy began when our children were small and continued with varying shades of intensity until we bought the Mill. Lloyd and I had read about experiments in Utopias. I longed for escape from economic pressure, for a way of exchanging goods for labor, for avoiding the use of money. I did not want to surrender to my load of adult responsibility without exploring alternatives; but I did surrender. For years while the children grew, my time and energy were consumed surviving. Now I could live in two worlds. The swamp on our Mill property became our Walden Pond. "Both place and time were changed and I dwelt nearer to those parts of the universe and to those eras in history which had most attracted me." I had found the rural simplicity of my dream.

We dodged sparrows nesting above the doorway leading into the concrete side. Crows moved into crevices near the corner where our new roof met the cement wall. Mice crawled down the space around the stove pipe, and cats entered through the unfinished roof. We were neighbors to nature by having built next to it.

Back in the city I read books and watched builders. But all of my craftsmanship is apprentice quality. The brick I laid under the stove isn't level and the hinges I installed on the bedroom cupboards are inside out.

In total however, Thoreau might have accepted the Mill.

> I sometimes dream of a larger more populous house, a vast, rude, substantial primitive hall without ceiling or plastering, with bare rafters and spiders...A house which you have got into when you have opened the outside door...where you can see so necessary a thing as a barrel or a ladder, so convenient a thing as a cupboard, and hear the pot boil and pay your respects to the fire that cooks your dinner, and the oven that bakes your bread...and perhaps you are sometimes requested to move from off the trap-door, when the cook would descend into the cellar, and so learn whether the ground is solid or hollow beneath you without stamping. I might visit in my old clothes who lived simply in such a house as I have described, if I were going their way.

Our eclectic skills flourished. The first Mill acquisition was a padded chiropractor table we bought for $13. Stephen and Mike found a tall shoe shine chair at Deseret Industries, worrying it would be sold before I made the purchase. Lloyd approved a round wire book rack and two hundred paperbacks to fill it. Subsequent thriftstore excursions yielded prints of Bruegel, Picasso, Van Gogh, Renior, even a Grant Wood already mounted for two dollars.

When the roof was finished the second summer, we decided to add a "loft."

"We're not going to risk lives," Lloyd said in the morning, eyeing the forty-foot drop to the west and south from the rooftop. We had prefinished the three hundred pound walls in prone position before raising and connecting them. Stephen lifted and Lloyd hammered while the rest of us balanced the walls with attached 2" x 4"s. No one had lunch until the second wall was secure. When the third wall was in place we yelled and took crazy pictures, then quit, hoping the wind wouldn't blow until we came back the next weekend. But Stephen seldom returned after Labor Day that year; he was a sophomore in high school.

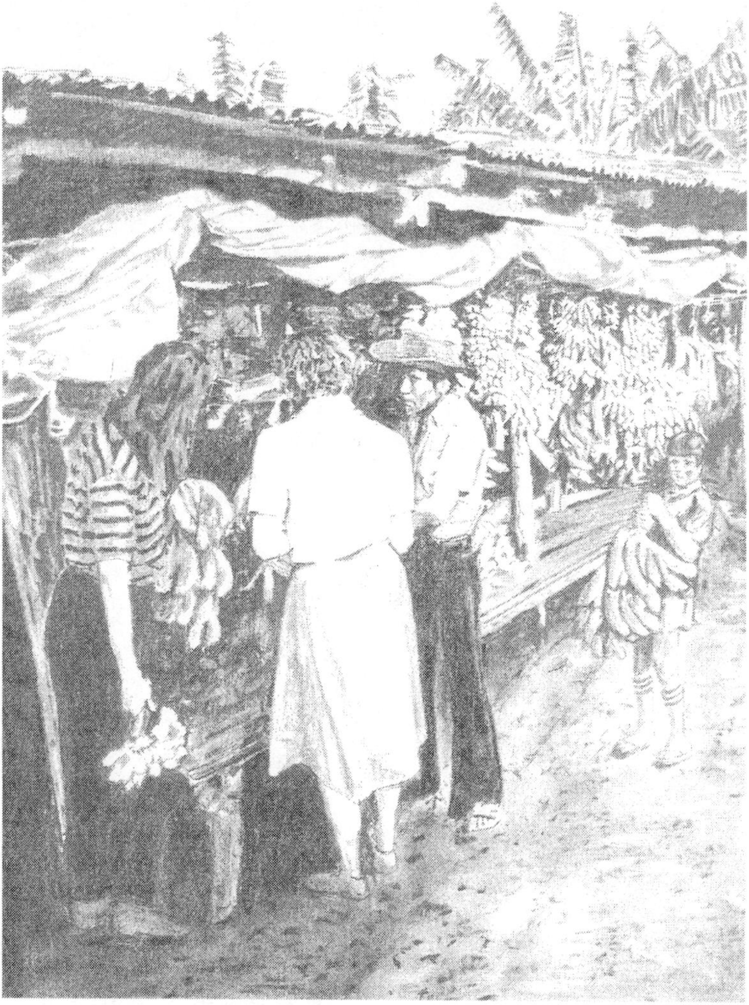

three

Mexico

I volunteer at a children's orthopedic hospital.

Each month I cover a four-by-sixteen-foot section of cork board in some appealing way that utilizes the talents of the child patients. During the autumn before Stephen's death, my daughter Martha helped me shorten the world map to fit into the long rectangle, eliminating the poles, condensing continents onto green butcher paper.

Children in the hospital colored pictures of people in their native costumes from Japan to Alaska, copied from a teacher's aid publication. I counted them—fourteen pairs which, spread out, would make a nice showing on the paper world.

On the day we mounted the display, all the patients left for their wards when dinner arrived, so Martha and I finished stapling the land masses onto the blue paper ocean. We had skipped cutting out Malaysia and the Pacific Islands, even the Philippines. The board was getting too complicated.

"Now's the artistic part," I said. "Stand back and tell me where to place the figures. It must be educational." The top half of the map filled quickly. Europe was overcrowded. We had to put the Greeks in northern Africa and the Irish overlapped the Dutch.

"That's all right. Europe is overpopulated," said Martha. "Let's add animals next week. It's okay, Mom."

It was lifeless and imbalanced. Maybe if the figures had bordered the map or banded the world like an equator? I was thwarted. Most of the world's people were not even on that map at the hospital. What kind of teacher's aid packet of international figures had no Arabs, no blacks, no Chinese? How dare we fill the empty spaces with animals?

That September I was reading the journal of a black woman who had lived in the slums of Sao Paulo, a *Child Of The Dark*. A worker had asked her, "Is it true that you eat what you find in the garbage?"

"The cost of living forces us not to be squeamish of anything. We have to imitate the animals," she said.

This black woman had to watch her daughter smile because she didn't know how. And she had cried for her children when she smelled good food in a neighbor's house.

"September 14" she wrote: "Today is the Easter of Moses, the God of the Jews. The black is persecuted because his skin is the color of night. And the Jew because he's intelligent. Moses, when he saw the Jews barefoot and ragged, prayed asking God to give them comfort and wealth. And that is why almost all the Jews are rich. Too bad we blacks don't have a prophet to pray for us."

I can't remember when I first became aware of inequality in the world; I expect when I saw it in Mexico at age twelve.

When my businessman father became an educator, he insisted on month-long vacations. We traveled into Mexico in our navy blue DeSoto; we slept in cheap motels with cockroaches. We ate packaged bread topped with goats milk spread and drank bottled mineral water. In Mexico City my parents took us to eat at Sanborns, where the food was so spicy it made me sweat.

We had walked by the open market stands of baskets, pottery, and leathers next to smelly fish, meats, and fruit buzzing with flies. We bought only papayas which we could peel, and bread we could find in *panaderías*. We watched women grind corn and bake tortillas on the street. Father also took us back into the dark warehouses where men blew glass and soldered silver all day. People walked along with us trying to sell their wares, trimming the price on goods Mother didn't want until Father would buy, only to find things cheaper in another shop down the street.

"I didn't believe he could go any lower and make a profit," Father said. He was holding a silver filigree necklace and earring set in his hand. "Think of the labor."

We returned to our parking place. A young boy stood by it with many friends, all wanting to be paid for having guarded our car. Those boys were about my age, didn't have shoes and didn't ride in cars.

As a parent I learned in one evening that my child was not aware of people beyond our provincial world. We had just moved to Tennessee and I was playing catch with my oldest daughter, Liz, on the grass in the front yard trying to avoid the cement horse trough that had been filled with dirt to make a planter box. We shortened our throws in the fading light. There was no reason to go inside. School hadn't started and Liz was lonely, self-conscious, and anxious about going to high school in Williamson county.

"Think of the future," I said. "Don't you want to travel someday?"

"No."

"Nowhere?"

"No, I'm really more comfortable at home." I looked to see if she was irritated at me, but she was content. The muggy warmth persisted and fireflies lit up the bushes.

"My parents thought travel was education," I told her. "They saved for trips."

"I save for clothes."

The porch light went on. I started to sit on the sticky grass but remembered about chiggers and sat on the edge of the trough with Liz. We were quiet. This daughter was sick on holidays. I had thought it was extra sugar or her excitable nature, but that night I reasoned that she reacted adversely to change.

Franklin High School broadened Liz. By the principal's office was a glass-enclosed correction room with paddles mounted on the wall. A third of the students were black. Liz thought they were disciplined more often than whites and that they enjoyed assemblies more, too. The day a jazz band came to perform Liz said, "The blacks were dancing in the aisles and up on the stage, Mom. They were more fun than the musicians." Liz didn't get sick on holidays anymore.

I realized our family needed to mix with a different culture to function better in our own. We purchased a used motorhome the year after we moved back to Utah. Square, like a cargo truck, it slept nine. Orange and gold mottled carpet with nubby brown upholstery reminded us it wasn't fashionably new, but it had power and size. We planned a three-week vacation into Mexico, researching at the library and talking with experienced travelers.

Several hours past the Mexican border we stopped near Monterrey for gas. The ground was muddy and children ran out of our way, standing barefoot beside the fuel pumps. We walked into a din of foreign voices. A group of men surrounded blond Martha. "*Los ojos azules*," they kept repeating. I listened until I could comprehend that Martha's fair coloring would create such interest.

The road atlas assisted us into Mexico City on Avenue Insurgentes to the Museum of Anthropology on schedule, but leaving was impossible. Mexico City was under construction; no detour returned us to the route we were following. After two hours we saw a line of lights on the highway leading east, up by the volcanoes toward Veracruz, and we couldn't drive to it.

"The maps are worthless," Liz said. "Let me take a taxi and lead you." Liz pointed a driver toward Highway 180 and climbed in a VW cab with twelve-year-old Stephen for protection. We followed helplessly behind the red bug carrying our two children.

The Yucatan was a conglomerate of palatial ruins and modern shacks diffused in tropics teeming with snakes and oversized insects. Climbing down the back side of the Temple-Crowned Pyramid at Uxmal, clutching a hot safety chain, I was unable to see anything beneath me but open space three hundred feet above the ground. I imagined human sacrifices on the altar beside me.

"The Mayan priests could have had my blood," I shouted, "before I would have walked down these steps!" Lloyd and the children coaxed me a step at a time.

We stopped at roadside stands for pineapples, avocados and bananas. We chose the biggest of everything. "No," the owner said. He was standing by the large bananas and pointed us to smaller ones. We bought the big ones, the whole stalk, thirty two of them. They turned out to be a bland cooking variety. The small ones were sweet.

In the fishing village of Campeche, a group of Mexicans who were with us in church asked to see inside our motorhome. Liz wanted to please them; she rushed in ahead to straighten up. The guests followed and thanked us politely when they left. Liz came out last, dejected. "It's nicer than anything they have, isn't it?" she said. We felt guilty to have camped the previous night amongst their sheds.

We caught barracuda off the coast of Isla Mujeres. Our native guide had ugly scars on his back from a previous excursion when a fish got loose in the boat. He cut the fillets out for our supper. The boat owner explained that our guide would take the bony parts home to his family.

Leaving Mexico City the second time, on our way back to Utah, we moved in gridlocked traffic going a block an hour.

"Why do these people put up with this?" I complained. Parallel to us, peering in at us, was a busload of natives going home from work. They were jammed together in the heat for three hours, eyeing us fixing and eating our dinner. They continued to stare while we washed the dishes and pulled down the beds. I was troubled with a traffic jam, an accepted and minor element of these people's lives. I turned off the interior lights in our vehicle, trying to hide.

Mexicans disclosed to us our provincialism and their patience. We noticed disparity in El Paso on the trip home, in New York City the next summer. We began to recognize it in our own neighbors—the people living under the viaduct in Salt Lake City.

Stephen examined inequality closely. During the September when I was drawing paper animals to complete the display at the hospital, Stephen was selling raspberries on the roadside near Logan.

He came to me early one morning. "A man is sleeping in my room and I don't want you to be afraid," he said. "I picked him up by Paradise and I'm taking him back up to sell for me today. He's interesting, Mom."

Mr. Bernard came in from smoking in the yard while I was frying French toast. He had a black patch over his right eye, tan jacket, trousers, shirt—even a tan Stetson.

"I like your place here, Madame," he said. "I've traveled all over and I've never met more friendly people. Your son's a fine example."

Mike and Martha hurried into the kitchen to eat, dropping their school packs on the sideboard.

"Try Spanish on him, Mom," Mike said.

"I'm a Frenchman," he went on, "but I know Spanish, not as well as German or Italian. I have always found languages easy." Stephen smiled at me. Yes, this man was interesting. Mr. Bernard had eaten two bites of his first wedge of toast. The high school students left and the younger boys came in to eat wearing their night clothes.

"I have this philosophy," he said. "Enjoy every day and don't worry, don't rush around. People get so busy they don't enjoy life."

I looked through the kitchen window at the laden apple tree while birds fluttered around the upper branches, pecking at the ripe fruit, set off by the blue sky. I could sit there and enjoy the view, but the children would be late for school.

"That man was about to snake my raspberries and $40," Stephen said the next morning. "I hope he gets a little wiser. He spends everything he has and doesn't save a thing. In fact Bernard is lazy. He would have slept all day and not earned a cent if I hadn't kept checking on him."

"Are you glad you picked him up?"

"Definitely. He taught me much more than he could have taken."

During the following winter, Stephen wrote to a brother who had been too young for the Mexican vacation. "I think I want to save up my money and leave the country. You and me only know what it's like to be rich. I think it would be a shame not to know how the majority of people live."

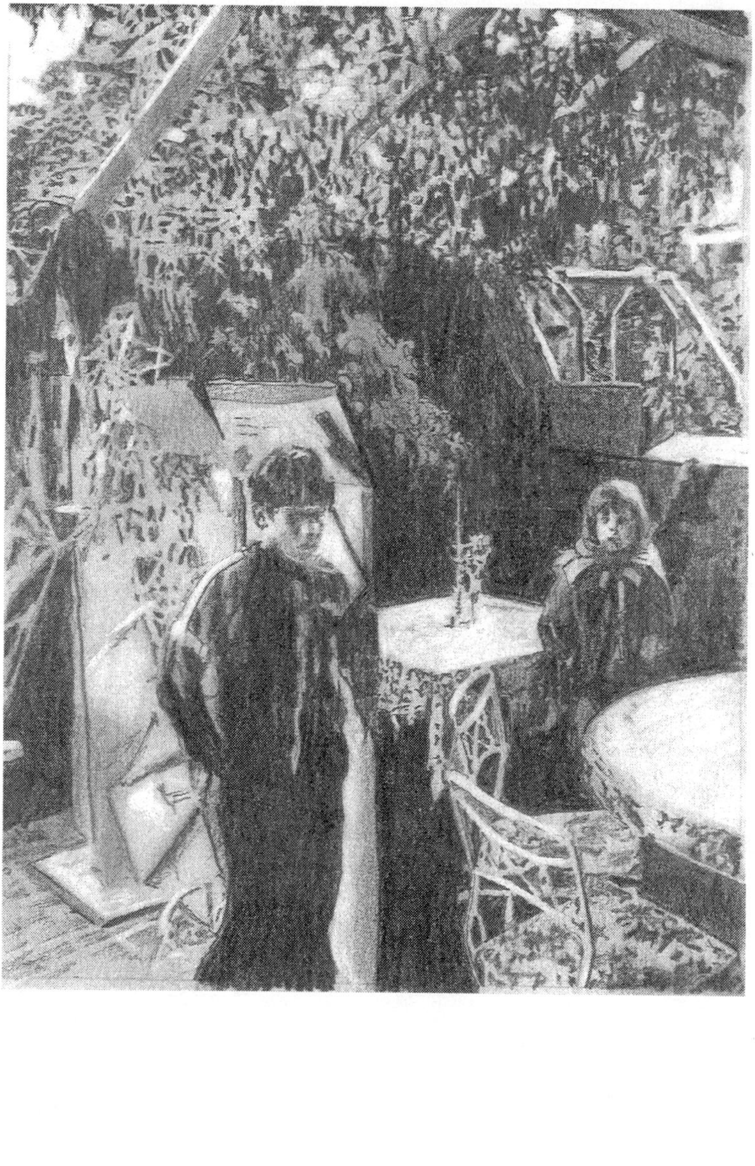

four

Emily's Story

This book is not a biography—Stephen wouldn't like that—so things creep into it that affected all of us. There are nine children in our family and this chapter is about the third one, born three years before Stephen.

I saw the adoption placement attorney for the first time in California when he took me to get our three-day-old Jewish baby. He was Jewish too. He drove fast and quietly except for the occasional clink of his metal hook knocking the steering wheel.

The birth mother had checked out of the Van Nuys hospital the day before. In the clear plastic nursery cart I imagined our baby looked like my two other girls, confirming our decision. It wasn't until I was back home and saw her with them that I noticed her darker complexion and larger eyes.

She was being adored in the middle of our bed that evening when we decided to name her Emily, envisioning that she would write verse. Her natural mother had a job copying manuscripts for a writer.

My father was the first of our relatives to visit Emily. He followed us alone into the bedroom to see if her nose looked prominent. Father had worked ten years for a Jewish investment firm on Wall Street. Two days earlier he had told me, "I have great respect for Jewish people. If you feel you should adopt, don't hesitate on this baby, but don't tell your mother she's Jewish."

I was born in New York City. I recognized "Jewish" in kindergarten. Jews were the ones always talking. They played on the stairs going to recess, blocking others. I had never tried to pass them but just watched, listening to their loudness, amazed at their nerve.

Holding my new baby, I thought her Jewishness would be forgotten or diffused. We didn't hide her adoption or focus on it but presumed she was supposed to be ours like our natural offspring. I was learning how to parent and I didn't see that parenting Emily was different than the others.

When Emily finally walked at eighteen months, she danced—curly hair flying, dark eyes frenzied with happiness, jerking wildly; often family and friends asked to watch her.

"Her movements are peculiar," Mother said. "It's instinctive."

"What nationality is she?" a friend asked. "Do you know?"

We moved into the home of a Jewish widower when Emily was four. Mezuzahs were still on the door frames, dishes were left in cupboards and embroidered shawls, furs and ornate jewelry remained in boxes. All of our girls were thrilled with more costumes; Emily kept the clothes in her closet.

Every day she dressed-up, body whirling, absorbed in movements she hadn't been taught, reviving in me the realization that her progenitors danced around Torah scrolls. The California attorney had told us that the birth parents were active in the synagogue.

Emily had a low, infectious laugh. She made friends with strangers, mesmerized animals and dramatized stories under the spruce tree. She said prayers with confidence that God's heaven was within speaking distance. She was loud and bossy and our family got along better when Emily had her own room.

By age five Emily was preoccupied with finding her identity. I stood at her door late one night while she looked in a magazine. A cache of *Better Homes and Gardens* lay in a pile by her bed. She kept turning pages while I waited.

"I'm looking for my 'real' mother," she said. "I think she looks like this." She showed me a picture of a young woman with long, dark hair bending over a baby in her arms, which she would cut out and tape to the wall in her room. I scrunched down on the floor by Emily's bed to be closer to her. I was troubled too.

Emily's birth mother had located us. Five years earlier, before leaving the hospital in Van Nuys, she had directed the California attorney to place the child for adoption. But she had never signed the papers relinquishing her baby. The California attorney told us the woman disappeared so we had posted abandonment notices in a Los Angeles county newspaper when Emily was nearly a year old, before completing the adoption. After years with no contact—when this forty-one-year-old woman was married to another man, had two sons by him, and was suffering from emphysema—she traced Lloyd to his office. She wanted to see Emily. Every year she called back, hoping we would relent, but she respected our belief that meeting was not right for Emily, yet.

Emily calmly kicked soccer goals from center field and

jumped horses at the steeplechase outside Nashville, yet she screamed over cars left running in the driveway and babies sitting on sideboards. Liz and Emily yelled at each other a lot—Liz, with her oldest child authority and Emily, unable to take orders from anyone.

When Emily was twelve, we sent money in her name to help build a memorial park in Jerusalem. Back from Tennessee the next year, it seemed important to celebrate the Jewish holidays with our family even though no one else, including Emily, knew about her Jewish heritage.

A neighbor, active in the Kol Ami synagogue, gave me a calendar before Rosh Hashannah, also a recipe for honey bread shaped like Jacob's ladder to sweeten the New Year ahead. We had no Shofar or ram's horn so Stephen's friend came with his trumpet to "open the scrolls of our lives to examination."

The eve of Yom Kippur we lit candles at dinner and took turns asking forgiveness for offenses to each other. I imagined the crowded synagogues. The next evening we started building our sukkah from two refrigerator boxes. We propped them up on the patio with the swing set and buttressed them to the roof with 1" x 4"s. Lloyd trimmed the olive tree; the children piled limbs on top until it looked like a tree house. They decorated the cardboard walls with ivy, cornstalks and squash from the garden. The rest of the family was delighted but Emily stayed in her room, uninterested, obsessed with her differentness. She only came out for meals.

The psychiatrist said that contact between an adopted child and the birth mother is usually disastrous, but "you may have no choice." Emily had grown to hate me as the barrier between her and her roots.

Emily didn't dance anymore but she played the tambourine for Hanukkah. We sang "Shalom" and lighted candles on a menorah.

Lloyd and I planned a trip to southern California alone. Adoption had taught us that we didn't own any of our children. I wondered if we needed to give Emily back for her own good.

We met the birth mother and her husband at a family condominium near Dana Point. She gave her two young sons directions for cooking frozen pizza before we left for the Crown House Restaurant. Both she and her husband wore white suits. He was a mechanic, born a Baptist.

"She used to cry at night for the child," her husband said. "So I told her, 'If it will make you feel any better, call them!'" The mother shared escargots with me before dinner. She was friendly and scared and reasonable. I liked her, this frequent nightmare in my life. She was a strong, protective parent. For eight years she had called Lloyd at least annually. That spring Emily was fourteen and went to meet her Jewish birth mother.

Emily came back from the trip to California confused. Passover festivities had been limited to unleavened bread at normal meals. Emily and I sat together on her bed talking into the night. She wanted to know about our Passover feast, the way it says in the Book. "What did you have besides Matzdah?" she asked. I told her about the sips of grape juice, parsley and lettuce dipped in salt water, boiled eggs, and mixture of apples with nuts before the leg of lamb. "We opened the front door," I said. "Your chair was left for Elijah."

While Emily had been in California we told the other children about her Jewish heritage, blending cultural, religious and practical definitions. After the seder banquet we had talked about the Old Testament Jews, the stories of Moses, Daniel and David that they knew. Our neighbors were examples of Reformed Jews. Then we got out photographs from our trip to Israel to show them the Zionist Jews, those on the kibbutz in Galilee and the Hasidics by the Wailing Wall.

"Is that why Emily's skin is darker?" Mike asked. "Jews aren't a race." I said. I knew there were blue-eyed, even blond Jews. By then we were so confused that I quoted Rabbi Kertzer, "We believe in God—a personal God...whose reality makes the difference between a world that has purpose and one that is meaningless." That definition simplified all the others; Emily was still like us.

"What kind of Jew is Emily's fake mom?" Stephen asked. He could not understand why Emily wanted to have another mother when one was plenty for him. I paused, tangled in his question. Suddenly I didn't feel like a brave adoptive mother anymore. I was comforted by his loyalty.

The following summer Emily went to California for two weeks. Her birth mother lived in a small house on the desert. The husband was a chain smoker, the mother was on oxygen and Emily was developing serious asthma reactions. On that trip, she told me, her birth mother slapped one of her boys when he acted up.

Now, when the mother called on the phone for Emily, she talked to me too. I was desperate for any help I could get. Emily continued to mature, dangerously insecure and pretty.

The next spring Emily's birth mother died. At the funeral the Rabbi read a poem that Emily had written. Honored as a child, Emily poured dirt on the coffin with the two younger boys. The traditional stone was left by the side of their mother's grave; they burned a candle for the three days of mourning. There were no flowers and lots of alcohol. Eight months later Emily left us, and moved in with her "birth family" until eventually she was hospitalized for bulimia and depression. After a year and a half away, Emily stabilized and moved back to our home. She began to develop confidence in her individuality.

I wonder what it's like to quest for identity. Watching Emily search I saw how crucial it was to know about one's progenitors. It wasn't enough for me to know and respect her background; she needed the perspective herself. And only if we all knew, and could discuss it openly, would I be able to clean out my hidden prejudice. Undercover I had vacillated from pride in her heritage, to purposely forgetting it, or blaming the Jewish stereotype. Albert Einstein understood that human tendency. "If I am right the Germans will say I was a German, and the French will say I was a Jew; if I am wrong the Germans will say I was a Jew and the French will say I was a German."

But the Jews survive, they flourish, and so did Emily. They are a mystery Herman Wouk struggled to define. "So strong is the identifying strain of Hebrew descent" that, he concludes, "descent or faith determines who is a Jew."

Emily is an integral part of our family and she is still Jewish. After she called her aunt and uncle in California during the '91 Iraqi war, she told me, "I just needed to know what Jews are thinking, Mom."

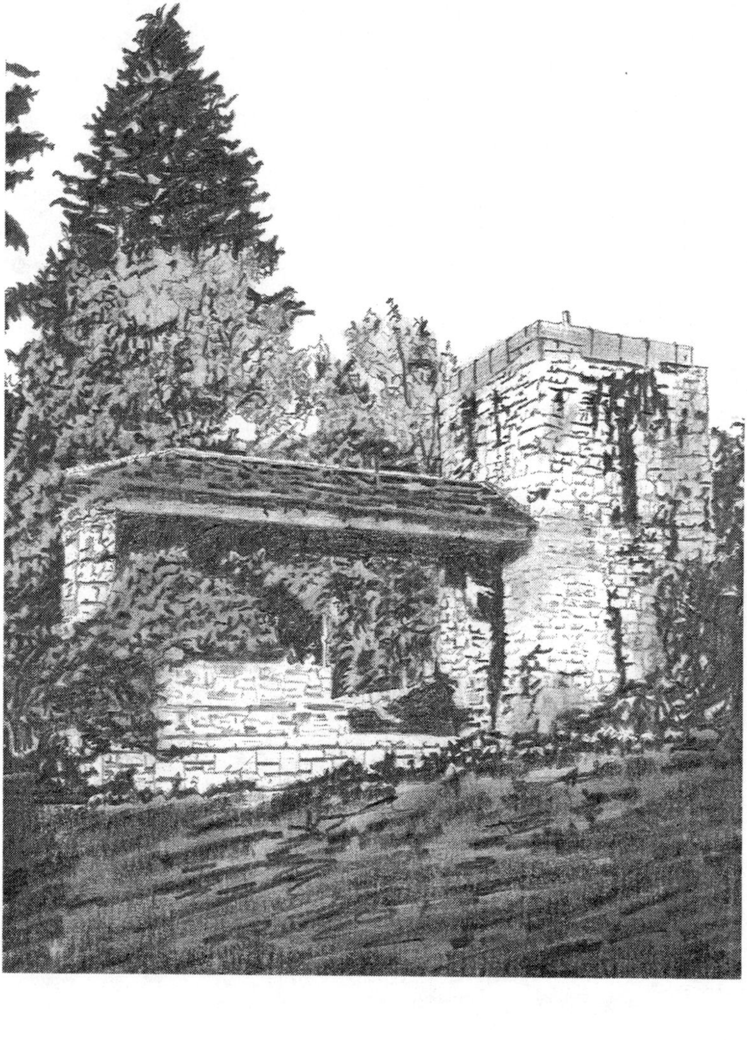

five

The Stone Fort

Facing a defiant child, I learn what principles I cannot abandon. The encounter is painful. My child is defining the boundaries of his freedom by pitting all his strength against mine. Our passions match but inside I feel torn. I know the risks; my child might forsake me.

When Stephen left to pick pineapples in Hawaii his junior year in high school, he said, "I have to get out of here and find myself. No one understands what I'm going through."

"I do!" Emily said. She had married at eighteen, three weeks before she graduated from high school.

Emily arrived at the Mill Saturday morning, the month before Stephen left, and quietly took me aside to explain that

41

he had hosted a party in our home the night before. Even though she and her husband were sleeping on the downstairs sofa, Stephen had walked into the family room with a group of friends, already quite drunk, to watch a video. Not only was Stephen legally underage to drink, but drinking was a violation of our family's moral standard. He resisted Emily's new adult role.

Soon after, Stephen learned of the Maui plantation that supervised students. "Don't stop me, don't tell anyone but our family," he said. "If I wait until summer I won't have the courage to leave my friends." I spent the afternoon shopping with him for a trunk, rain gear, army pants and zinc oxide. He scheduled a physical exam before he had to be at his job at 5:00 P.M. I had a Spanish test I needed to study for that night; I felt like I was being pushed around. Lloyd was out of town.

"Don't buck the change you've been hoping for," a friend said. Stephen left the next morning and Mike followed two weeks later.

Mike stayed on to finish his contract in Hawaii but after three months Stephen was sent back; he had stolen alcohol. It was recovered untouched but Stephen rebelled against doing endless jobs to compensate for his action. He arrived home the last day of school. Stephen taught swimming lessons and did lifeguarding until it was time to sell raspberries. He helped put up the kitchen ceiling at the Mill and hiked Timpanogos Peak with the family, always struggling against me over curfews and drinking.

"You set your own curfew," I said. "I'll meet you when you come home."

At midnight I was lying on the sofa in the living room dozing when Stephen came in laughing with friends.

"Mother dear, they drove me home so I could be on time," he said. "We haven't cut the birthday cake yet but I'll be back in half an hour." I fell asleep waiting.

Another night Lloyd was restless, sleeping on his study floor when he heard someone tapping on glass. He watched in the dark as a figure ran back to a car in front of our home. A few minutes later Cathy, the quiet one just older than Stephen, ran out the door. It was 1:00 A.M.

Michigan Avenue and 2000 East had been labeled "Pizza Corner" two years before we had any clues. Neighborhood teenagers met for pizza deliveries in the summer darkness long after reporting in to their parents.

"You don't want to know everything your teenagers do," my son-in-law said.

That summer Lloyd and I took turns being with the younger children at the Mill. One of us was always back home at night.

I arrived in Salt Lake City on the first Friday in August at 9:35 P.M. The phone rang at 9:55. "Mrs. Poelman, I have your car in a parking lot on Wilmington Avenue. Can you come over?"

The maroon Honda our teenagers shared was parked next to a construction truck, both gas caps were off, a new coil of plastic tubing lay on the ground. Stephen and his friends had not started siphoning yet. The car's front door was open and the interior light revealed Stephen's wallet on the front seat.

"They ran up across the street and into the park. There were three of them, do you know the other two?"

I looked up where the policeman pointed, through locust trees obscuring a steep embankment—a street light illuminated the lacy, bug-eaten leaves. We were in the shadows beneath, two police officers and myself, and no one seemed to be in a hurry.

"We have two choices," the shorter one said. "We can arrest them later tonight or we can let you handle it, this time." The owner of the truck, who also owned the parking lot and the adjoining building, had already been notified; he agreed to have the boys work for him instead of filing charges.

The tall officer leaned against the side of the police car. We talked about teenagers.

"Know where your son is at night. It's your right—tell

him. He's underage."

The shorter one stood by his open door half listening to radio messages.

"Lady, either you handle your kid or the law eventually will," he said. "Split them up, they're no good together."

Lloyd and I had increased responsibility. We were no longer just imposing moral law on Stephen; now we were confronting civil law.

Like Augustine as a teenager stealing pears, Stephen didn't need the goods. The gasoline wasn't as important to him as the thrill of acting against the law.

I accepted the facts but I hardly recognized my son. Driving to the Mill two summers before, the same Stephen said to me, "Guys who steal ought to be jailed. It's not fair. Their parents don't know what they do—they're hypocrites!" And I said, "Don't worry about them. Justice prevails. They're not caught...yet."

Stephen and I stood by the back door after the first day of his senior year in high school. In the morning he had met his friends by our garden fence, the first time I had seen them together since their meeting with the truck owner.

"Even the police demanded that you split up," I said. I had relaxed my own judgment during the past month. Following the direction of officers with authority was a relief.

"But Mom, we'll always be friends," he said. "No one can stop that."

Stephen had told me his sophomore year, "There are very few people I want to be with. The rest are guys whose mothers buy their clothes, or they're the hard druggies." He had found friends who craved danger and dared each other on.

I sympathized with Stephen's point of view but I couldn't give in.

Stephen moved into the stone fort, an old guard house at the entrance to the golf course. Access was through an arched wooden door that dragged across the rock entry. Inside the

8' x 8' room of cemented stone, walls extended up twenty feet to a metal roof. Two narrow openings allowed light through steel bars. The place smelled of urine—police periodically boarded it up when they discovered vagrants living there. Stephen carted in a mattress, sleeping bag, lantern and scraps of carpet. Lloyd and I crossed the boulevard at night and walked by quietly—faint light shone out through the tower which looked like a jail. No one noticed except those of us who knew. Mike and Cathy walked over too and Stephen let them in to talk.

My father visited Stephen there, as did the social worker, and finally, in late October, the young man who used to give him rides on the motorcycle. Stephen had been using our electric heater which he attached to five hundred-foot extension cords that went through the trees, down the hill, across two backyards and plugged into the side of someone's house. "It's freezing Stephen," the young man said. "Come live in my brother's room until Christmas."

I don't know how to prevent youthful defiance but I know what it feels like. I helped Martha as she worked with a white filly that ran like Pegasus in the field. Wearing a soft red halter the young horse fought with all her strength; two of us could not budge her. A week after Stephen's funeral, I felt like the filly. I wanted to break loose from the sorrow dropped on me.

"I'm going to get my hair cut and my ears pierced," I had told Lloyd—daring action for a conservative mother. "Well, wait until you see what I decide to do," he said, responding to my belligerency. He was baffled and so was I.

That afternoon I went to Ear Gear with Martha. She assisted the clerk in measuring for the perfect position of the studs. I had no hesitation, no speedy heartbeats, but calmly stepped over the line of deep-set opinion.

In third grade at Wasatch Elementary, I knew a girl who had her ears pierced. She lived in a dugout, one of those dwellings where only the basement was built. All you could see from the street was the door in a triangular frame going into the ground. She wore her hair curled high on top, long and flat in the back, with her ears always showing. She had strings through her earlobes that looked like dental floss which she wore for months before the tiny gold rings appeared. Some of my friends said she was a Gypsy. That sounded primitive to me.

Our teenage daughters had started asking for piercings years before. I had been appalled. They wanted to distort their bodies! I visualized the cover of *National Geographic* with the African woman whose ear lobes hung down to her shoulders, dangling plate-size ornaments.

When Emily moved to California, she went to the mall the first weekend for piercings, in open defiance and excitement.

Cathy, just younger than Emily, wanted them just as badly but she waited, impatiently, until age sixteen when even I acknowledged it should be her decision.

Liz and Stephen had their ears pierced about the same time; Liz was twenty-three and Stephen seventeen. Stephen's technique was typically creative and economical. He used my darning needle. Later, while he was working for a T-shirt company, Stephen shot a plastic tag holder in his ear. The cardboard part dissolved in subsequent showers but the plastic remained for nine months until a police officer cut it off.

Martha had asked to have her ears pierced while Stephen was living in the stone fort. "Yes," I said. She looked puzzled. I had retreated. I was letting go of my preferences in the face of a determined child—conserving my energy, my rapport, for critical issues. We went to the store that afternoon. Michael, just back from the pineapple plantation with Clorox-bleached hair, accompanied us to tease. "Why spend your money on pain?" he asked. Martha sat on the stool while her ears were measured, pale and clammy. I wondered if she had wanted me to say "no."

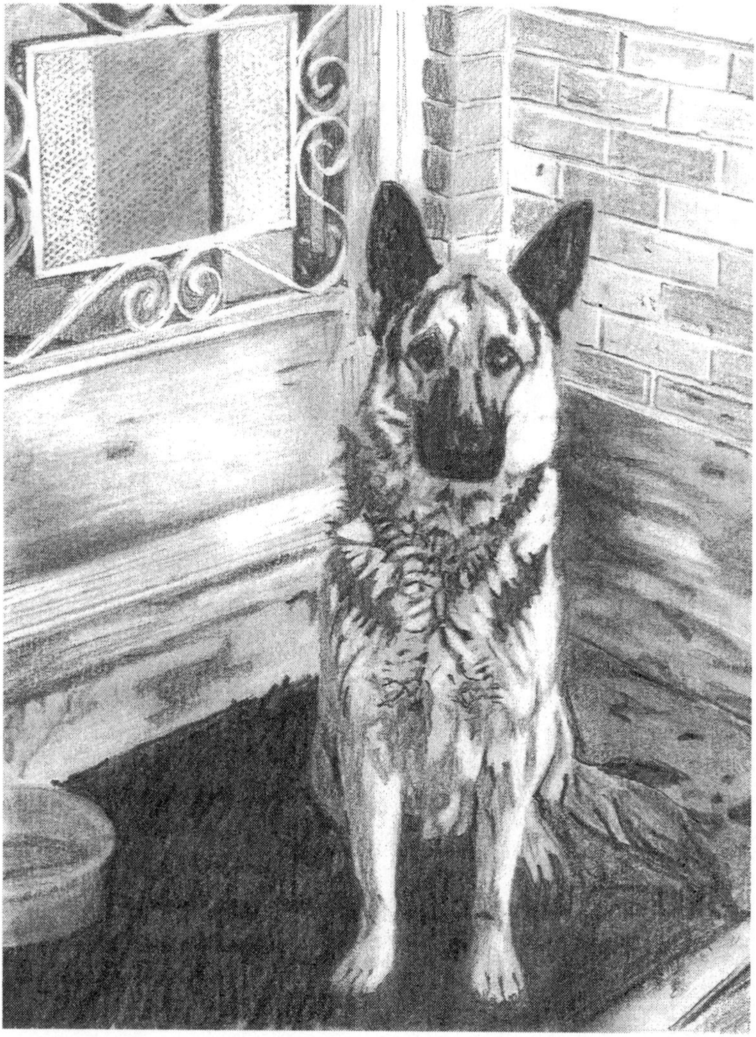

six

Dogs

I heard the rusted iron gate grind against its latch. There was no wind. I lay alone, watching the lines of light around the bathroom door; Lloyd was showering. Our dog was loose in the yard, entering through two wrought iron fences. I worried about how much he might damage.

Last night when I heard the dog enter, I jumped up and knocked on the window calling into the blackness, "Go back, Hogan!"

Cathy had found Hogan shut in the shed one afternoon. She put him back in his run. That same night she returned, stood in the garden and watched the German Shepherd walk through bars in the gate four inches apart. Hogan had previously forced the welds loose on both gates, lifted the latches, and opened the shed door.

Fifteen years ago we decided to get a big dog. We had been vandalized during Christmas week—teenagers cut through the window on the back patio door while we were away. They smashed musical instruments, figurines and the gingerbread house on the dining room table. Salad dressing and eggs were thrown the length of the living room at paintings and mirrors. They stole all of our electronic equipment.

In the spring we bought Tosh, a Golden Retriever. He occupied the area along the fence by the apple tree, across the cement court, to the yard grass. He went to dog obedience school with Emily. She was underage for the class but was admitted because of her determination and commanding voice. Cathy cried. She had similar dark eyes and hair, but was rejected for her soft voice. After a year, when Tosh could retrieve and heel, regular training stopped. The children wrestled with him on the front lawn. Lloyd jogged with him across the street to the golf course. Some mornings, Tosh wouldn't come home with Lloyd; I was left to stew and take him to the vet when he had eaten nylons or plastic sacks out of the neighbors' garbage. Tosh was tied to the garage door when Mike pushed the automatic opener. The dog hung there, yelping and kicking while Emily and Cathy lifted his bulk, screaming, until he was lowered to safety.

I cried when Tosh died unexpectedly. He shivered in the summer sun and wouldn't eat—antibiotics couldn't save him. The vet threw the ashes away.

We channeled our grief into a quick replacement from the Animal Shelter—a one-year-old Great Dane, already papered and named Barkley. This dog looked intelligent, lounging and sleeping in human poses. He had a pet rock that he pushed and chased, snarled at, and struggled to carry in his mouth. Every day he played privately with the rock and always, when someone noticed him, he put on a demonstration. When Barkley lost a rock we went to construction sites or up the canyon for replacements. Fiercely protective, Barkley attacked anyone he thought was hurting a family member. He bit a friend's shirt off for pushing Mike.

As Barkley's knees weakened, his temper around strangers became more unpredictable. On the night of Emily's wedding, he bit one of the serving girls. Weeks later he bit a jogger.

Each trip to the vet revealed hopeless bone deterioration. We disguised aspirin in food scraps for him at meal times.

Lloyd and I went to California for a weekend and came home to an additional dog. Stephen had borrowed money from his younger siblings to augment his savings, totaling $85, and he bought a German Shepherd from a litter advertised in the newspaper.

"That dog will have the perfect home, the most love, the best training you can imagine," Stephen told the owner, "and that's all the money I have."

To me he said, "I need a dog to run with. I'll train him, feed him and pay for his shots."

That night Hogan slept in Stephen's bedroom without my permission. Stephen had covered the floor with newspaper. I found the excrement a week later in one corner behind the bed where the newspaper didn't reach. Two months later, Stephen left to work in Hawaii. The little Shepherd bit at the knees of aging Barkley. The Great Dane had to be put to sleep. I saved Barkley's collar on my dresser for when Hogan was big enough. Cathy helped the younger ones bury the ashes under the blue spruce.

Stephen wrote to us about the vicarious dog funeral he and Mike held for Barkley in Hawaii. They buried his photograph, a rock, and a can of soda pop, topping the mound with a cross and a hibiscus blossom. Then they set off three fire crackers and sang "God Be With You Till We Meet Again."

"German Shepherds are vicious! Get rid of that dog. He's

not safe with your children!" said Martha's flute teacher. She told me of a German Shepherd that had been carefully trained by her neighbor in California. "She'd had the dog seven years and one day it took a little girl's head in its mouth and wouldn't let go. The neighbor had to give the dog to an army corps."

I looked at John, our six-year-old son, and tried to imagine his head in Hogan's mouth.

"Get rid of him, Mother," my married daughters said. "We can't trust him near our babies." But dogs had remained part of the family just like our children, no matter what they did.

Stephen wrote to me, "My dog is the most important thing in my life. I'd die for it." He sent me money for Hogan's shots. I knew we needed to socialize the dog; that would help make him safe. I made sure that Hogan went places—to baseball games, to the shopping plaza, and on walks around the neighborhood. When children played with him, he snapped back and I worried. People only forgive a puppy. But love for Stephen meant love for his dog. Hogan stayed.

In the fall, when Stephen was back and living in the stone fort, he came by to play with his dog, but it was Mike who signed Hogan up for dog training at the armory. Each week Mike practiced with Hogan and attended class. Hogan was the star pupil. The night Hogan received a cardboard crown and certificate of achievement, Mike fed him a chocolate cupcake.

The next session was inside during cold weather. "The scent of the other dogs is too distracting," Mike said. "We did fine until this white female came." The dog "drop-out" couldn't heel.

Hogan was tied to the lamp post while the boys threw a football in the front yard. Our policeman neighbor came over in the evenings to pet him—he wanted a dog just like Hogan.

Stephen was back in Hawaii when we noticed the seizures. The children screamed one morning while watching

Hogan out the kitchen window. The dog was lying on his side foaming at the mouth, his legs stiff and thrashing. We ran outside and watched until he calmed, glassy eyed, and slowly turned over, staggering to his feet. Pie-shaped blood stains marked the spot. Each morning we looked for evidence of more attacks and found it about three times a week. "It's common in dogs," the vet assured us. "If it gets too bad, we can consider medication."

When Stephen came back the next summer we took Hogan to the vet together. The medication for seizures was expensive and would need to be given twice a day with no guarantee of results. "Hogan's danger is hurting himself during an attack. Keep his area clear," the doctor said. "He may grow out of it."

Stephen was disappointed when he took his dog running. "Hogan doesn't keep up with me," he said. "Good thing I never let you have him neutered."

I left for the Mill Sunday night, December 23rd, in the new van together with the younger children, presents, food and a tree tied on top. Lloyd followed in the old van with lumber for the new stairs and Hogan in the kennel. The temperature was below zero heading east. Lloyd got a tank of bad gas near Park City and sputtered along; we arrived in Evanston after 10:00 P.M. While we heated soup at B & B Quick Shop, Lloyd let Stephen's dog run loose. Hogan's water had frozen so Martha and I filled his bowl in the restroom and carefully carried it out. Hogan was missing.

"Animals die in these temperatures!" I said. Lloyd drove to the west through dense housing. I circled east around the railroad tracks and warehouses with car windows down, calling, whistling. At 11:00 P.M. we stopped a policeman and registered our loss.

They found our dog. Stephen and Mike picked him up at the pound as they traveled through Evanston Christmas Eve. Hogan was a camel in the nativity play. He was not well cast but he performed obediently, asleep before we sang "Silent

Night." There was one dog fight that night. Lloyd put Hogan in his kennel about 3:00 A.M.

Christmas Day Hogan bounded behind the snowmobile, weaving across the boys' snow boards as they glided and jumped. Christmas night we took turns breaking up dog fights. Hogan wouldn't stay in the kennel and he didn't fit in with the rural gang. In the morning, as Stephen prepared to leave for Salt Lake, I pleaded with him to take his dog.

When Stephen returned in the spring he asked me if I really liked Hogan. "Yes" I said. "He's calm, no problem, no evidence of seizures." Stephen waited for me to say more. I couldn't. I was Hogan's caretaker but I sensed he didn't think that was sufficient, even for a dog. Mike told me Stephen had found a new home for Hogan in case we felt he was a burden.

The day Stephen died, he spent time in the back yard. I expect he said good-bye to Hogan before he left. The next day Hogan drooped. "He knows something's wrong," Emily said. "Dogs always sense these things."

I wonder about dogs. They often make me feel guilty. Hogan will sit on the cement for hours, head erect, and look intently at me working in the kitchen, generating an ambiance like the beasts in the Book of Revelations. Sometimes I want to close the blinds. He knows my weaknesses. He's only entered the house three times in his life and each time I escorted him out with boldness that distressed me. When I pull weeds around his dog run, he'll sniff at my crotch until I get angry and boot him away. But he's a friend when the fence separates us. I pet him each time my arms aren't loaded, partly for Stephen, sometimes six times in a morning's gardening. It's a sham though. When I take scraps out for him to eat on the back porch, I pet him distantly, suspicious he'll lick me and make me smelly.

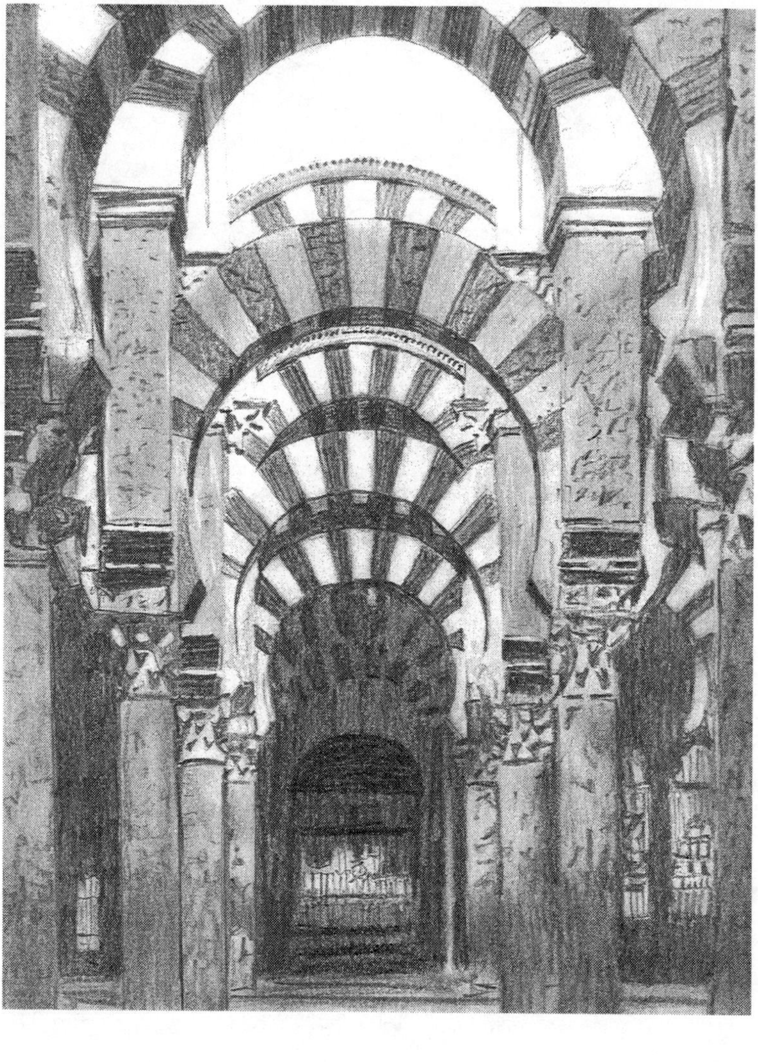

seven

Traveling

In front of the Spanish Consulate in Madrid, I zipped my reissued passport into the nylon pouch given me three days earlier and tucked it next to my skin. Liz's boyfriend, Frank, nodded approval.

"Use the pouch for your valuables," he had said in the car to Lloyd and me on our way to the airport in Salt Lake. During the transatlantic flight, Frank shifted the contents of his wallet into the pouch which hung around his neck. "I was told it's the only safe way to travel," he said. That was his style, make suggestions but don't push anybody. I had worn my pouch empty to show appreciation. But I already had a purse. After our passports and airline tickets were stolen, I followed his example.

A month before the trip Frank had called me on the phone. "The advice I'm getting from my friends is not to go with you and your husband to Spain," he said.

"Do what you think best," I told him, "but your friendship with Lloyd and me is separate from your relationship with Liz."

Our open communication with him evolved, and continued without interruption, though he never married Liz. The first time I met him was at our kitchen table around a pot of soup. He and Liz had gone snowmobiling for the day with Mike and Martha. A hat had matted his hair oddly, his glasses kept slipping down. He discussed current issues with us as he spooned down two full bowls. Once he paused in his conversation to say, "The soup is quite good." And I said of him that night, "Well, if Liz marries him, it will be for character." Early in their acquaintance I had interpreted his lack of pretense as naiveté and my teenage children thought his genuine interest in them was intrusion. We changed.

When Liz went to Spain for eighteen months, as a missionary for our church, Frank came to dinner often and spent holidays with our family, always initiating personal conversations with everyone.

"How is the 'U', Cathy?" he said. "How is your social life?"

"Why is he interested, Mom?" Cathy asked me when he had left.

Stephen and Mike went fishing with him at his ranch. They talked about investments, land, inventions. The boys were elated with ideas, relieved that Frank wasn't trying to impress them for Liz. "He wouldn't even let us keep the fish we caught. He said, 'We've got to protect the future.'"

Frank was equally ready to light fireworks with the children on the Fourth of July, build a redwood deck at the Mill, and discuss parenting approaches with Lloyd and me. He negotiated with me to share the take from his elk hunt—

"I'll do everything, if we can split the meat and packing fee."

In years he was just older than Liz, but by professional experience, middle-aged. His father, fifty-five years senior, had been Frank's best friend and business partner until he died on Liz's birthday a year before her mission. His mother had died from an allergic reaction to penicillin when he was three. The well-trained young man inherited the responsibility for three businesses—a cattle ranch, a plastics plant and a growing subdivision. His increased professional status didn't affect his apparel. In Madrid he wore new galactic jeans and a sea blue sweatshirt, presents his brother had received for Christmas and wouldn't wear.

We agreed to travel together without an agenda or reservations, as frugally as possible. We made many mistakes on the trip but it wasn't because of Frank. He was asleep in the back seat while we ignored his earlier cautions and drove past Bilbao to historic San Sebastian where my travel book erroneously showed the rates were cheaper. He negotiated in fluent Spanish for the hostel and led us back when we were lost, having memorized the address. He located the mission home in Bilbao through a series of phone calls after I discovered that my bag containing the address was still at the airport.

The first night my husband shared a room with him, adjacent to the cubicle where Liz and I stayed. The experiment was not repeated. Lloyd was the only one who slept, snoring. Liz and I told stories in the dark, lying in twin beds, laughing and talking until morning. When I was young, my mother and sisters instinctively cried during departures and arrivals, while reading good books, and when they were very tired. I had watched them and waited for my own similar response but I never made tears.

For our reunion celebration, we ate Chinese food together in Salamanca, a city built in Carthaginian times and made famous in the Middle Ages by Arabic scholars. I cautiously refused to leave my purse in our room or the car but totally forgot it in the restaurant. Lloyd and I returned ten minutes later and it was gone. When Liz and Frank arrived to help communicate, waiters, cooks, and cleaning boys in white coats lined up shaking their heads, then led us back to the kitchen where we sorted through dirty table cloths before going to the police station.

At 1:30 A.M. we followed a uniformed escort through narrow halls, up two flights of stairs, through several offices to the constable in charge. The room was dark with one lamp lighting the desk. He took from file drawers six long forms and put them on his desk, one at a time, before looking up to us for information. I had lost all hope that my purse would be found.

I bit my tongue as the serious inquiry over my cheap mail-order purse took place. A wave of giddiness, untamable when exhausted, built inside me. I looked down, trying to stifle my frivolity. One glance at Liz doomed us both.

The official heard our disruption.

"*Salgan*," he ordered.

In the outer office, we exploded in laughter and were escorted farther away near the stairs. The men joined us half an hour later, appalled. "What's wrong with you two?"

I was sorry. I hadn't committed a crime. It wasn't that important, was it?

I was satisfied that I was learning something from losing my purse that justified the evening. I vowed in the silence of the ride back to the hostel never again to criticize my husband for carelessness. I even forgave him for losing the money that had fallen from his pocket in Florence twenty years ago and the clothes he had left in the dresser in Rome on the same trip.

The next day Liz's purse was stolen from our Hertz rental car. The wing window was smashed while we toured the university founded in 1230 by Alfonso IX. The oppression of the Inquisition hung on the richly-adorned facade of the original building. Tapestries and carvings decorated the halls outside stark classrooms and the guarded library filled with precious manuscripts. The privileged students were bright-eyed, as they walked briskly to classes past our car.

The clutch in the rented Jetta was giving out—metal scraped as the gears shifted but it ran adequately at constant speeds. We started back to Madrid for a car replacement by the scenic route, around the turreted wall of Castillian Avila.

"Brother Poelman, do you have suggestions on driving?" Frank asked. "Brother," an accepted title amongst church acquaintances, now sounded as remote as "Lloyd" had been intrusive when Frank began helping us at the Mill three years ago. Pulling off the weathered exterior wood for wainscoting in the main room, Frank's ladder had leaned on the second story as he jerked at the nails. "Lloyd, here it comes," he called, and then my husband caught the loose lumber. I was pounding subflooring with Liz.

"I can't stand to hear him calling, 'Lloyd'," I said. "It seems so disrespectful." I realized I had been raised by a generation conscious of titles. I wasn't sure I liked the inheritance but I didn't repress it. Liz talked to Frank. He never used our given names again.

Liz's friend was unaware that familiarity could be offensive, not because of conceit. He seemed oblivious to Lloyd being older and unaffected by the fact that Cathy and Stephen, or any of our children were younger. He talked to John, the ninth child in our family, with as much respect as to me.

Frank let Liz drive into Madrid. She wanted to despite awful sounds with the clutch. Lloyd was a nervous wreck in the back seat, hesitant about Liz or me at the wheel. Lloyd asked him to drive again.

"I could," he said, "but I don't want to take it away from her." He manned the emergency brake at every stop so Liz could continue.

That night we walked the brilliant streets of Madrid. Marquees flashed "Rainman" and "Rocky III" in the winter sky. Throngs of people wore black or brown; leather, gold chains, and furs added variety. We didn't see families in the

metropolitan capital like we had passed in the Salamanca and
Bilbao darkness. They were singles walking, youth out to
discover what Franco's powerful dictatorship had kept hidden from their parents under the facade of a liberalized
regime.

We slept in the cheapest hostel of our trip that night, four
of us lined up in our sweat togs on cots with thin mattresses,
equally miserable. The tiled room was cold with a naked light
bulb hanging from the ceiling. The bathroom had no hot
water, just a leaking tap to mingle with the city noises. I
promised Frank I would roll Lloyd over when he snored.

The next morning, we found three heated rooms. Walking
in Buen Retiro park in the afternoon, Lloyd and I bought four
cuttings of a root from an old woman, imagining sugar cane
which we chewed until Liz and Frank rescued us—
lightheaded, our mouths anesthetized. When we returned to
our new rental car we patched another broken window with
cardboard, which held for the rest of the trip.

Further south in the winter warmth, we entered the
mosque in Cordoba through a patio bordered with orange
trees. We wandered through a myriad of marble columns that
supported striped and scalloped arches, opening into vast
domes crowned with Arab filigree work and Byzantine
mosaics. The mosque was finished in the tenth century, the
grandest of 3,000 mosques built during Cordoba's height as
the center of Moslem and Jewish culture. Ferdinand III
conquered Cordoba in 1238 A.D. and decided this mosque was
too great to destroy. So he commenced building a cathedral
inside the mosque. We had been walking around for half an
hour before we arrived in front of the doors to the cathedral,
part of a huge bulk looming up incongruously in the south end
of the Islamic masterpiece. A native guide told us about
Catholic Charles V's visit, decades into the progress of
construction. The builders asked him, "Isn't it beautiful?"

"A cathedral could be built anywhere," Charles said.
"Here was the one great mosque!" Frank had heard the same

account when he visited there three years earlier. The story was not in the brochure we purchased. I admired Charles V's honesty. I trusted the story. Candor had redeemed our trip.

I sat next to Frank on the flight back. As he awakened he closed his mouth smiling. "It was pretty wide open, wasn't it?" he said. "I had something funny happen once," he went on. "I fell asleep on a bus with some kids coming home from a field trip in high school and they stuffed my mouth with wrappers, paper clips and all kinds of junk. It was pretty awful."

I marveled at this man who carried no personal illusions; I had come to believe his appearance elicited trust.

"Have you thought of getting your adenoids checked?" I asked. I had told Liz my theory on why he always breathed through his mouth, and I was sure she had passed the observation on to him.

"Yes, but I'm so busy," he said. "It doesn't seem that important, does it?"

eight

The Porch Light

Stephen came to dinner occasionally after he moved away from the stone fort but he wouldn't be found on Thanksgiving. He had gone golfing. The morning before Christmas, on our way to the Mill, we looked for him on Michigan Avenue. Cathy had heard he was staying with one of the "pizza corner" friends to elude us.

Cathy and Mike went into the neighbor's house first. After twenty minutes Mike returned. "He feels that if he doesn't live with us regularly, he doesn't deserve to come with us on holidays," Mike said. Martha talked with Stephen next, "We've never been separated on Christmas!"

John, the smallest, went in last. "It's my turn to give to you this year, Stephen," he said. "What if you're not there to open my present?"

Lloyd had turned the motor off; the vehicle cooled as the children went in and out recounting the conversation. Lloyd and I sat quietly, looking at the frozen front yards all the way down the street. Cars passed, throwing ice at our tires. People waved.

"Stephen'll go if he can first have time to bake treats for his friends," Cathy said. She stayed to help him, assuring us they would drive up together.

We tried to accept the difference in Stephen that holiday. He had drawn John's name as well, giving him a batting target—green cloth stretched over an aluminum frame with white Velcro balls. He received warm things: boots, battery operated wool socks, gloves and an alpaca hat. By 6:00 P.M. Stephen was jittery, desperate to leave. Cathy offered to drive him back to Salt Lake. He was used to drinking to subdue pain in his fractured collar bone and temper the cold as he rode his scooter to school in the snow. After New Years, when I came home from the Mill with the younger children, Stephen had moved back into his room.

Our family was snowed in the first Sunday in February. It was no disappointment to have our regular church meetings canceled because the chapel furnace had frozen. A drift banked the northwest corner of our front porch, flocking the hall with snow each time the door opened.

We spread out in the living room for a discussion while a turkey baked. Lloyd was talking about Christ's life when Cathy said, "I think the challenges today are harder than in the days of the Savior."

"No question," Stephen added, "there are problems now that weren't even invented back then."

"But I've been out there in a battle," Liz said. She had been home from her mission less than a month. "Every issue is a struggle between good and evil. That struggle is as old as the world." The discussion circled around the room; everyone was enlivened by participation. Liz and Stephen kept it moving.

Stephen wore a holey khaki sweater and red Converse high tops. He was comfortable. He shaped as forceful a case for his opinion as Liz did for hers. Then he went to his room and put on a fresh shirt for dinner.

He had been on Prosac for two weeks. A doctor friend sitting on the stand at church during Liz's homecoming talk observed him on a folding chair back in the hall. "I see in your son what I saw in myself before I got antidepressant medication, and I don't like it," he said. "I've invited him to talk to me." Stephen made the appointment. "I can't concentrate," Stephen had told me. "There's no way I can do well in school."

He decided to go back to Hawaii the next day. Lloyd was frustrated. "There's nothing for you there now, Stephen."

"There's nothing for me here! I hate the cold, you know that," he said. "I'm doing poorly in school. I know how to work—I know I can get a job."

After that conversation Lloyd helped Stephen prepare to go and I did nothing. My emotions were used up. If Stephen wanted to go I would not interfere, but I would not help. He checked out of school on Wednesday and left with his trunk, backpack and guitar.

When he arrived at the airport in Maui, he stored his things in a baggage area and started out on foot to look for work. He called home a week later from Rainbow Ranch.

"I take care of the horses," he said. "There's a little shack they let me sleep in—it doesn't cost me a thing." By then three of us were on the phone. Stephen started laughing, "I'm happy, you guys. I've got my guitar."

Stephen finished high school in Hawaii through correspondence courses. On rainy days, flooding forced him into the barn with the rats. He became a guide on horseback for trail rides. He asked Lloyd to send him more Prosac. Every day he practiced his guitar.

He owned a red electric Fender that he bought when he was fourteen after passing off the last of fifty hymns, a prerequisite to graduation from piano in our family.

Lloyd and I had gone with him to the music store. Stephen was ecstatic. "Isn't it the coolest?" he asked. The guitar was plugged in and Stephen played a chord holding his fingers down firmly while he moved the whammy bar back and forth. I looked at Lloyd. How could we veto such enthusiasm for music?

I vibrate to music! My parents had allowed me to learn an instrument besides the piano, too. The only stipulation for me was that the orthodontist approve it—none of those instruments that he said would accentuate my overbite. I chose the French horn. I could imagine making sounds like the hunters in "Peter and the Wolf." Music adhered to my soul the day of a combined high school band concert. The French horn players were seated on a raised platform looking down on the rest of the orchestra. We played "Finlandia." My unsure tone was bolstered by ten others blasting out the opening chords; I ended the piece blasting as loud as I could. I knew French horns were the most important instruments that day and that spirit never died in me, but stayed in my memory, often as distinct and living as during the high school concert.

"Yes, Stephen, go for it!" I said.

Mike got a drum set for his thirteenth birthday. Lloyd and I bought a used amplifier for Christmas and a bass guitar which Cathy learned. Rebecca, our second oldest child, arranged the music and played the piano, Martha the keyboard. The first number they performed with Stephen was "Head Over Heels" by the Go Gos. Lloyd and I were ushered into seats on the sofa in the family room. Our children were making music together! We cheered.

All rock n' roll stayed downstairs. The living room was reserved for classical music and Lloyd was learning to be very broad minded. He had played the organ when he was thirteen and would have preferred a family orchestra.

• • •

After four months of hard work at Rainbow Ranch, saving all his money, Stephen was lured from the rent-free shack to an apartment in Lahaina by a wealthy Texan boy whose father owned oil wells. "I could go into business with him," he said on the phone. "The wells are idle—the oil is just sitting there."

The Texan also played guitar. They bought a volume pedal together.

"Don't worry, when I'm not studying business reports, I practice. I'll be home for Liz's wedding."

Stephen played heavy metal. I was still adjusting to U2; the first time I had seen the name on a T-shirt in the wash, I hid it. "That's mellow," Mike said, "nothing like what Stephen plays now, Mom." In my mind heavy metal was not music, but some kind of modulating anguish.

In the middle of the night, Stephen telephoned from Los Angeles. He had wanted his arrival to surprise us. Transferring from the airport to the bus station he was mugged. In the wedding pictures his black eye was not noticeable; Martha toned it down with Maybelline Concealer.

Cathy, who was then the oldest living at home, sat with Stephen and Mike in the family room after the guests and bridal couple were gone. They were exuberant to have another sister married.

"First, we have to decide who gets Liz's room," Stephen said.

I had hauled lugs of fruit downstairs used to decorate the serving tables. I thought the idea had been economical. To prove it, I couldn't waste a single apricot or cherry. I had already broken a two-quart bottle of raspberry preserves on the floor in the kitchen, trying to stuff it into the refrigerator next to molds of butter, currant scones, and herb dip.

Stephen talked with his guitar in hand, picking out chords quietly without plugging in. During the reception he had stayed out by the Ten Penny, a group that played English folk tunes, even while he bounced Rebecca's baby to sleep in his arms.

"I'll keep my old room if I get the plaid sofa from upstairs. I want a studio look," he said. I sat down on the floor to listen, and decided I was too exhausted to object. As I went to bed, the sofa was being lifted over the railing onto the stairs.

The next day I took some of the fruit from the reception to my mother, who always feels privileged to be given produce for canning. My father was resting in the study. He explained the limits of his strength. "I can only stay up for three hours at a time," he said. "I can't live like this."

When advanced lymphoma was diagnosed, Father chose aggressive chemotherapy instead of the moderate option. Stephen kept careful track of my father's health condition. Father had listened to Stephen's business proposition: steerable innertubes—cheap, great for sliding, and potentially controllable.

"My idea will also cover the protruding valve," Stephen had told him.

"When you have it perfected, come to me," Father had said. Stephen loved my father because he gave up trying to change him and began helping him. Stephen cried at his funeral. He was a pall bearer.

"I'll bet Grandpa would have liked the alarm stickers," he said a few weeks later. Stephen had hundreds of them professionally designed and produced similar to those used by the chief security firms.

"For $1.50 you can protect our home, Mom. Choose your favorite style."

Stephen quit taking Prosac. He found me alone in the kitchen one afternoon.

"I can't stay on it—I'm an adult and I can't be dependent on something," he said. "It's not worth it. I don't want anybody's money wasted."

"Expense can't be the issue, Stephen. The doctor said to stick with it for at least a year."

"Mom, it's not the money, it's me." Stephen pleaded. "I've got to be myself!" In his mind, self-respect precluded medication and in my mind, his opinion mattered.

Stephen went to the university in the fall. He was most enthusiastic about his personal finance class. He worked part time to pay fraternity expenses and he sublet the sofa and half his room to a former neighbor who had moved back from New Mexico for college. In October, the night before his first exam, he took a study break. He went to Trolley Square to play a couple of video games with one of his old friends.

Stephen told me, "I watched the guy and said to myself, 'Oh no, here we go again.' I followed him into the back room where he took a sack of tokens."

I sat with Stephen in the dark at the dining room table waiting for the police to come. We could both see the lighted front porch through the sheer drapes. Lloyd was in New York taking depositions. He had called a few minutes earlier.

"Stephen needs to be careful what he says," Lloyd had told me. "It's better to work through an attorney later."

We kept looking out the window as we talked. "Are you saying I shouldn't tell the truth?" Stephen asked.

"No, but you didn't initiate the theft. Will you say you were following your friend?"

Stephen turned away from the window to face me. "I can't Mom, that's cheap. I'll just have to take what comes."

The officers had Stephen step outside. I went back in the dining room to watch. Stephen looked directly at the investigating officer, not with defiance, but with respect. Homer comprehended my state, "Upon her soul came joy and grief in one moment." They put handcuffs on my son.

"You can pick him up at the jail tomorrow morning," a policeman said, "and take him to the parole office."

I left the front light on and walked around in the quiet house. I prayed all night, hoping justice wouldn't kill the honesty revived in Stephen.

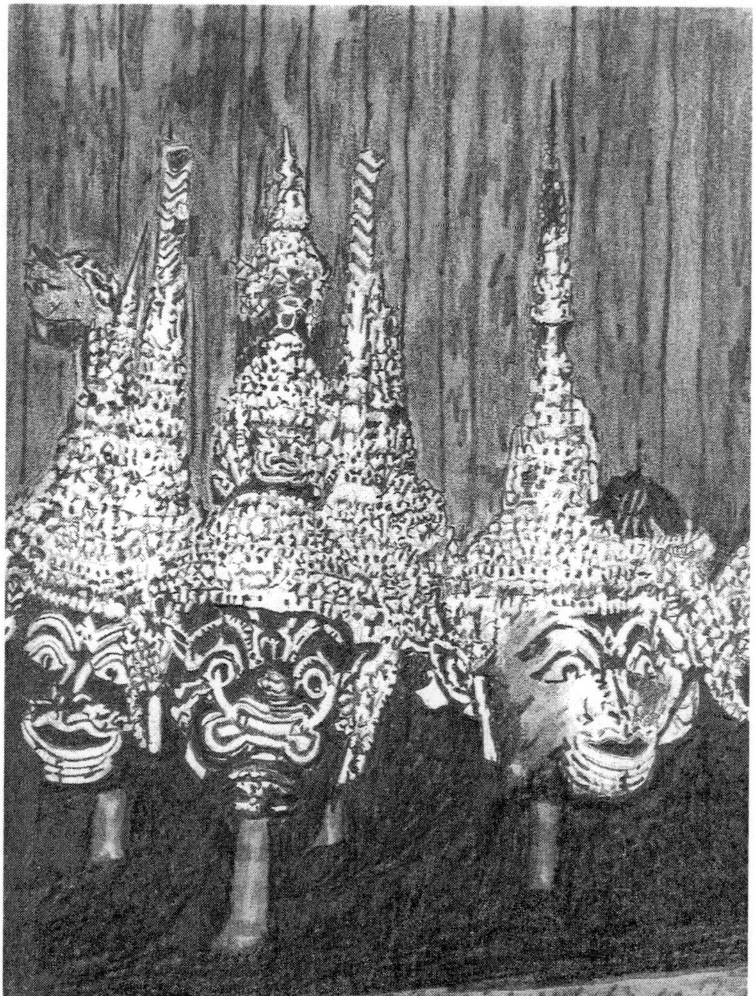

nine

Houses and Dances

"Who will finance my project?" Stephen asked. I kept wiping the kitchen table. I didn't want to involve others.

"It's hard to ask for money," I said.

"But this is a great deal!" Stephen wanted to be self-employed. He wasn't ready to return to the university yet. He listed all the businessmen he knew while I loaded the dishwasher. He didn't talk about approaching anyone but Frank.

"If you'll put up the money for a house," Stephen told Frank, "I'll fix it up for resale. I'll do all the work."

For Frank, who wanted to help Stephen, it became important to study the classified ads with him and bid on homes they agreed were a good value. On May 14, 1990, they made a purchase. It was probably the happiest day of Stephen's life. He was nineteen years old.

The house was a dirty, rundown, two-bedroom place on land overgrown with trees. There was no garage or carport, no appliances or connected utilities, but Stephen could envision everything that was missing.

"It's a good house," he said. "Just give me a month and it'll be worth three times what we paid for it."

He moved in with a sleeping bag, radio, and flashlight. He worked around the clock for forty-eight hours tearing out carpet, stripping wallpaper, dismantling the bathroom basin and toilet. From then on he slept intermittently, plastering, sanding, and caulking around fixtures. He painted the walls and ceilings white with a new electric spray gun, then spent days loosening the wood-framed windows stuck closed. The wallcovering around the stained tub was scrolled back and two cupboard fronts were missing. After a couple of days trying to match samples, he glued the wall with linoleum paste, poured a gallon of Clorox into the tub and declared the cupboards open shelving.

It was July when Stephen started on the outside of the house, scraping and painting. Neighbors let him use their hoses for drinking, rinsing off and sprinkling the small lawn. Mike went out to help build a carport. Stephen subcontracted linoleum and carpet laying. Like our Mill it was taking longer than originally planned, costing more, proving much harder, and it didn't matter. Stephen was in charge. He had a goal that transcended himself.

In the fall, after cutting down trees and planting sod he thought it was ready for resale but computations on the value of the home slowed him down. Stephen had not saved all the receipts; days of searching did not help.

"They must have been thrown away—I'll just have to face that too."

Selling was tedious. There were lots of homes for sale in the same price range, the weather was turning cold, an agent was considering it for rental property.

"I don't want to sell it to just anyone," Stephen said. "As I worked in those rooms, I imagined a family with kids playing."

Then a couple who really needed the home wanted to buy—a couple caring for an elderly parent in a wheelchair. They couldn't get approval from their credit union unless the price came down. "I feel really good about it," Stephen explained to Frank. They closed the deal making a modest profit. Stephen was content.

"I've learned a lot, Mom," he said, "and now I own the tools to do another house."

Stephen's house project reaffirmed what a man named Eckeo had proven to me ten years before in Tennessee—having a cause empowers one to carry through, ignoring disappointments.

At the Nashville airport I kept forgetting Eckeo was the one in charge—the five Laotian brothers acted the same, politely bowing. Eckeo's mother was four feet tall. She stood in a wrapped skirt and thongs with her grown daughter and the two young ones, children of another brother left in Laos. The refugees had crossed the Mekong River on a moonless night over a year ago, swimming four hours with the elderly mother tied to Eckeo's waist.

I wondered how they felt in the rental property the first night; at least it was clean. Boxes of donated clothing lined one wall next to a sofa. The kitchen had a table and three chairs. There were beds. We had huddled on the floor together on blankets, eating rice and apples, smiling a lot.

Thirty-eight Laotian families settled in Nashville that spring. Many had been part of the Royal Dance Troupe in Laos, performing solely for the king. During the year in a Thailand camp, waiting for sponsorship, the relief agency funded the making of new instruments and gold-encrusted costumes, reconstructed from memory. I was told the costumes would be shipped to Nashville soon.

For days I went with Eckeo and his family to get physical exams, Medicaid, food stamps, social security numbers and enroll the children in school. While we drove I taught them some English. They tried teaching me one-syllable words in Laotian, laughing so hard that I wondered if my tonal insensitivity sounded crude.

After a month Eckeo said, "You bring family to my feast. I good cook." The living room on Stainback Avenue was transformed. The kitchen table had been moved in and covered with a bright sheet, chopsticks and baskets of sticky rice. The Laotian family served my family large bowls of mild ginger soup swollen with vegetables, noodles and pork, then waited, watching us eat, spoon feeding our youngest children. We couldn't finish the huge portions. I hoped they would eat our leftovers.

Eckeo got a job at a Creole restaurant after much encouragement. "Everyone has a job in America," I said. When I picked him up from work he was sweeping amongst the cane back chairs in a starched white jacket.

One summer evening Eckeo called. I was down by the creek with Stephen and Mike viewing their catch of crawdads.

"Eckeo needs you," Emily yelled to me from the deck. When I answered the phone all I could understand was "Lady…help." I was disappointed that his English hadn't improved in the past three months. "Please, help," he said again. It was strange for Eckeo to be calling me. I tried unsuccessfully to reach Lloyd and friends in the refugee support group. I took Rebecca, the calm one, and drove for half an hour across Nashville. Past the modern skyline and outskirts of tenement housing, we exited to an old, constricted neighborhood. I was lucky to get a parking spot half a block from Eckeo's place on Saturday.

The air was thick and hot as we stepped onto the street. Inside chairs had been moved out onto porches crammed with people fanning themselves. It was quiet, no music blasting or children yelling, only hushed voices as we walked along the cracked sidewalk. The windows in Eckeo's place were conspicuously shut and covered. The door opened as we approached and Eckeo motioned us inside.

His family nodded respectfully from their positions. The sister and mother were by the kitchen door, the four brothers by the windows, while the two small children played somberfaced on the floor. Eckeo showed me the large cupboard draped with sheets where shelves had been removed to accommodate thirty ornate masks sparkling in the dimming light. The head pieces looked like miniature Buddhist temples, each one unique, portraying a different character in ancient legend. The masks were priceless to the Laotians; the neighbors had concluded that they were valuable, too.

Eckeo was fingering his lips. "You take," he said. I walked through the house. The back door was battered where strangers had tried to force entry the night before. The bedroom window on the north had been broken and was reinforced with flattened fruit boxes and cupboard shelves. The brothers each held an elegant sword.

"What can I do, Rebecca?" I said softly. She had intuitively organized me under stress before. I wanted to open the front door and shout the truth, "The masks are paper maché covered with spray paint and mirrors!" We stood. Eckeo's fear began to scare me.

I picked up two masks and Rebecca followed. We walked fast, quietly, to the van seven times, trying to forget the staring crowd around us. Rebecca didn't hesitate; she trusted me while I expected I was being irresponsible. There had been two knifings in this neighborhood the week before. I hadn't read the newspaper account but a friend in the refugee agency had cautioned me.

"We keep," Eckeo said. He was gesturing at the swords, their only protection—they looked ornamental to me. We walked away the last time in total darkness.

All the lights were on when I drove in our driveway. The

children came running out, asking questions, wanting to help. Stephen was excited about his highest record yet—eighty-five fireflies in a glass bottle—which flickered in one hand, as he carried a mask carefully in the other. Lloyd came toward me last, angry with fear. I had risked lives helping the Laotians' cause. I had ignored the cost to my family and I did not regret it because the result had been favorable.

I went to Eckeo's for dinner a year later. "I will fix you my special food," he said.

The scheduled afternoon I arrived at his place on time but he was late. The meal evolved from cupboard and pantry. Pregnant and over-hungry, I ached for the first bite. Tears accompanied the spicy delicacies as they burned their way down my throat. Mixtures of chicken skins, soft bone, old eggs and dark fiery beans fought in my stomach.

I looked at Eckeo, totally absorbed in his own eating. He wore a pink Izod shirt. New carpet was on the floor. When he finished he said, "I do not keep my job. I must lead my people." Eckeo's father had led the dance troupe in Laos. Eckeo had grown up in the palace and begun his training, like all the dancers and musicians, at age sixteen.

"How can you live?" I said.

"My people help me. They give me money because I am leader. See? They buy carpet."

Other Laotians kept coming in. The door bell was interrupting our conversation.

"Do you understand?" he said.

I understood that the meal Eckeo cooked a year ago had been tempered to please my American taste, and that now he wanted me to be pleased with his spicy food. I respected Eckeo; I smiled.

"I'll be there for the performance," I said. He smiled back and that was all—no bowing or palms-together reverence anymore. Eckeo was trying to perpetuate the culture of Laos, even make a living at it. He hoped the sacred dances of

Buddhist legend, never seen by Laotian citizens, would be appreciated by American audiences.

I drove my children to Centennial Park in downtown Nashville. Three large tents with yellow canopies were set up on the grass. The complicated instruments—brass gongs, sets of bamboo pipes and wooden drums—were on one side of the raised platform. The dancers were standing around barefoot on the grass in metallic costumes. Eckeo greeted me graciously in a white smock and flowing blue pants.

A standing, strolling audience gathered; most people watched for a while and moved on. Dances varied from fierce warlike encounters by the men, to graceful splayed hand and foot movements by the women. Eckeo was happy, so focused on the performance that he didn't notice the sparseness of the crowd. I was proud of him. I want to memorize why I was not as proud of Stephen's finished house. I think watching his mistakes at close range had obscured my vision. Stephen's new tools that cluttered the garage, our boom box permanently covered with a fine spray of paint, the missing ladder, were continuing irritations. The contrast between what Stephen expected to earn and the small amount he eventually pocketed was, for me, evidence of a poor investment. But most of all, I didn't support Stephen's enthusiasm for another house project. I didn't respect how much he was learning. Both Stephen and Eckeo deserved my praise; they were content with goodness short of their dreams.

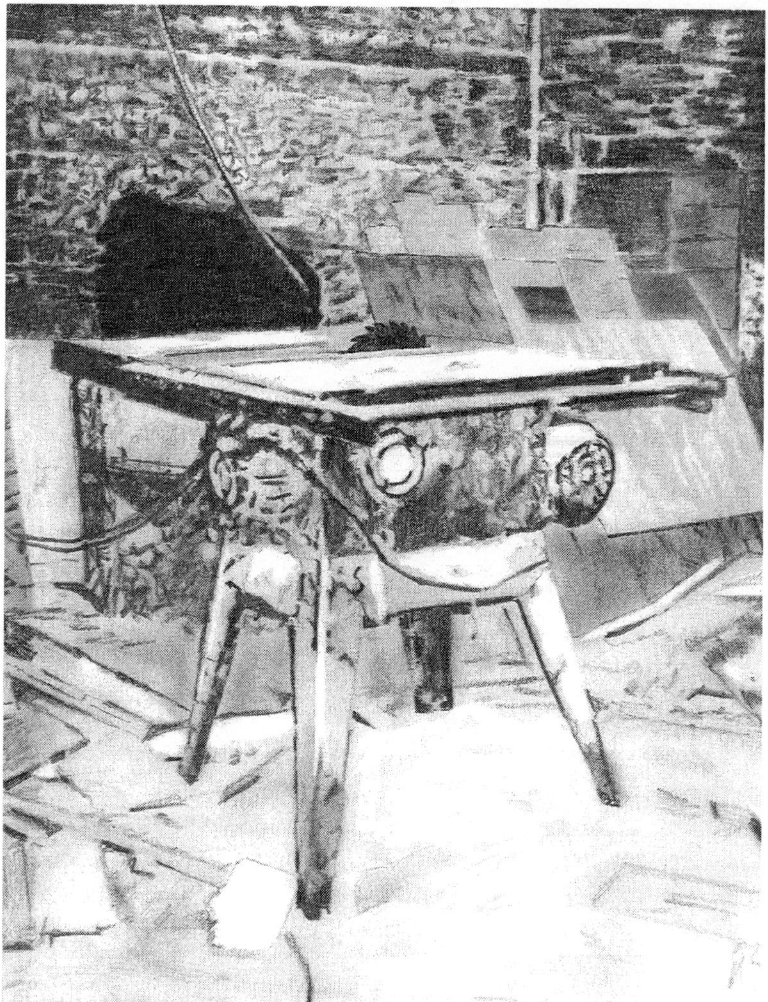

ten

Outbursts

"You are a mean one," my brother had said. "Just like a rubber band, stretch and pop." During my high school days, he awakened me when I fell asleep studying, and I yelled back, "Leave me alone!" "You're out of control," he said. "I'm sorry for your future husband and children."

I was frightened of the anger that came yelling out of me. Lloyd and I don't yell at each other. We disagree and discuss but it never erupts. With my young children, it was different. If I had asked one of them to do something pleasantly, then earnestly, the third asking was firmly. Depending on the distance of the child from me, or their stubbornness, the last request came out loud or very loud.

I yelled when I found Michael, as a baby, crawling into the street and Andrew, at age three, choking on a plum pit. Fear made me yell at my mother once. She and Father had come to the Mill the year they both turned eighty. They were self-assigned to cut and place the weathered wood as a diagonal wainscoting around the main room. Father chose each piece, measured carefully, and gave it to Mother to cut on the table saw. I worked close by, cutting out holes for switch boxes and turning the saw on and off. Mother's veined hands were tight on the wood, assuring perfect cuts. Near lunch time I watched as she put a last piece through the saw. She was relaxed. I marveled. The cut was accurate, her fingers guiding the wood past the blade. I turned the switch off and Mother grabbed for the cut piece, oblivious to the danger of the still whirling blade.

"No!" I yelled. Her hand slowed in mid air; she looked at me, unsure, defenseless. I had yelled at my mother, not when I was young, but when I had nine children and she had white hair! I was ashamed, not for protecting her fingers, but for having raised my voice with authority over her.

On a day in Tennessee when I was having mission zone leaders for lunch, the children couldn't find the box turtle, gerbil, and salamander, all loose in the house. When the children ran out to catch the school bus I yelled, "You can't leave me!" But I knew they couldn't hear.

Stephen and Mike had walked in the back door, reeking, after we moved back to Salt Lake. They had tried to catch a baby skunk by the golf course. "Strip and use the hose!" I shouted.

I don't like feeling out of control and I tried to diminish the outbursts. I learned to toss sponges to my children who spilled milk instead of raising my voice. I used lots of incentives—stickers on charts, treats—to cut down loud commands.

"You must not yell at Emily," the psychiatrist said. Our first professional visit had occurred when Emily was thirteen, after an impasse in the front hall of our home. She had been regularly going to a boyfriend's house after school where they stayed together until his working mother arrived. Emily was the physical equivalent of a fifteen-year-old and the boy was sixteen.

"You can't go there after school," I said.

"I will."

"Then you can't go to school."

"You can't stop me." We were both at top volume.

"It's wrong, Emily!" I shouted.

"You think I'm bad," she yelled. "You hate me!"

Emily ran out and I lay down on the floor. Our baby John crawled over to me, pulling at my nose and patting my cheeks. The other school-age children had slipped out quietly without saying good-bye and our four-year-old Andrew, the eighth child, was watching Mr. Rogers on T.V.

The psychiatrist prescribed no physical restraints, no criticism, and a lot of love for Emily. "She's very fragile," he said. I had to understand that Emily was scared too. The energy I used fearing her actions, being angry at them, must be shifted to controlling mine. The change seemed beyond my ability. Emily and I went from the psychiatrist's office to McDonalds and ate french fries together at 11:00 A.M. I took her to school after lunch, when she asked to go.

For days, after the children left for school, I lay on the sofa like I was recovering from surgery. On Sundays, I hoped no one would talk to me at church. I asked to be released from my assignment with the teenage girls. "I'm no example," I said. "Hang on," I was told. "You are, for some of their struggling parents."

There was a second impasse a year and a half later. Emily's birth mother had died but Emily was determined to move to California and live with her mother's husband and the two boys; she demanded the right to have an optional home. While she yelled, I concentrated on controlling the level of my voice, knowing our separation would need the bracing of my unconditional love.

That was the last impasse between us. Emily was tightly supervised in California. At her lowest point, she was linked up with a social worker she could trust. Emily learned to deal with her passions as I started to tame mine. We were becoming more reasonable adults, without killing our spirits.

Coming home from a counseling session together, a boy driving the car next to us got distracted looking at Emily and bumped into the car ahead of him. Emily looked away embarrassed. I watched, saddened. No damage was done. We could laugh two blocks later; someone besides us was out of control.

I didn't yell at Stephen during his rebellious stage and I only remember him yelling at me once. It was on the front grass of the house he was redoing after a weekend when we'd been away. Stephen had hosted a wild party in our home. Andrew, the younger brother he taught to play baseball, walked in on it. Stephen hadn't realized that Andrew stayed behind to play his league game. In the excitement of the party, Stephen sent Andrew to his room where Cathy found him later.

"I've been working for two months on this house project," he said "and I wanted a little fun."

"But that is our home," Lloyd said. "I work for it too."

"You'll never be happy with me," Stephen yelled, "unless I do what you want!" I encountered Stephen's anger and frustration. I was frightened and I could still think.

"Wrong," I said. "We want you to be happy doing what you want." I listened too. I saw the wet paint on Stephen's hands, the white siding with fresh gray trim by the front door. I saw that Stephen's abusing our home over the weekend wasn't the real problem. I ceased to push a moral standard on my adult son. He deserved to live with the consequences of his acts, free from my judgments.

Outbursts of passion command my attention; then I begin to reason. My personality tested the French maxim, "The passions are the only orators which always persuade."

Stephen moved back to our home the next week as he continued to finish his house.

When father died three years ago, I started visiting my mother regularly. Mother and I are girl friends now; we prune trees, listen to tapes and sort old photographs. Mother rides three miles on her exercise bike and does sit-ups regularly but I encourage her to take my arm in bad weather when we walk. I want to protect her.

The week after Stephen died, I kept our scheduled visit. As I made the hour trip, I thought about the anonymous letter written to me on the day of Stephen's funeral. The piles of sympathy cards had faded as I focused on a three-page handwritten censure. I had survived Stephen's death but I wondered how I would endure accusations that I had contributed to it.

It was addressed to Lloyd and me but my name was underlined, so I opened it.

> I ache for your family. I think crises happen and all we can do is learn from them.
>
> You must remember you choose to be high profile. You choose to be examples. You are rigid and make your children conform to save yourselves embarrassment. You had trouble with Emily and now Stephen—seek professional help.
>
> Stephen publicly committed suicide to call your attention to him. It was not God's will. It was not necessary. Do not settle for 'mission on the other side' idea.
>
> I know I'm being hard on you but my heart aches at this tragedy.
>
> —Stephen's friend and teacher

Lloyd wanted to destroy the letter. "It's not helping you," he said. But I couldn't leave it alone.

Driving to my mother's home I had tried to bolster myself emotionally to be with her. She is always praising me. She was raised by a mother who praised her and her siblings for

correct spelling, chores completed, and breathing, in addition
to specific accomplishments.

My mother opened her front door already speaking.

"Catherine dear, you're wonderful! I don't know anyone
who could handle this heartache like you are."

I stood on the front porch trying to stifle my emotion.

Mother started repeating, "Catherine, you're…"

"No Mother! Don't say any more," I yelled. "You're
talking to someone whose son is dead. I'm not wonderful!"

We were still at the doorway when an elderly neighbor
and her daughter ran over to us.

"We heard loud voices and just wanted to make sure
everything was all right," the older woman said.

Mother and I did little that day but talk and have lunch. In
the late afternoon, I spaded the small garden. We planted two
rows of beets and eight tomato plants. I apologized to the
neighbor and her daughter for frightening them, as they
worked nearby weeding their flowers.

I wondered as I traveled home if I had regressed to my
uncontrolled youth. I put all the windows down in the car and
let the wind whip my face and hair.

eleven

Driving

For the next week I composed all kinds of responses to the letter before writing the sifted ones on paper to the author whom I never found. I knew from experience that bad examples are as potent as good ones—whatever I was, I could help others. I scrutinized our past. Had we tried too hard? Did that create the impression that we "choose to be high profile?" Large families have more profile, I discovered from living in Tennessee across the street from country singer Marty Robbins and his wife.

Our home near Nashville was in the Bible Belt. Marty's wife, Mirazona, was Pentecostal. Down from her lived the secretary of the Southeast Baptist Convention. They ignored the missionaries we supervised. Missionaries were common in our neighborhood; lots of children were not.

"I thought this was an orphanage," Marty's wife said. Interrupting her gardening, she walked closer, "...all those children running out to catch the school bus by your 'Mission Home' mailbox."

When Emily was thirteen, I wondered if we had been overzealous to adopt her. In the days of decision following a miscarriage, we had sought to do our best. In spite of everything it would be ridiculous to regret those idealistic stages. I see other young couples striving and I say "go for it!" Living will temper the bliss.

When Emily was fourteen and our problems became visible, I learned that as I stopped worrying what others thought and did only what I felt was right for my child, the pain of being seen evaporated. That was years ago. The ache is gone. I cannot care what others think.

Still, the errors live in me. My errors while driving are worth remembering and I can talk about them now, since my son died.

Outside Chetumal, ten miles from the Guatemalan border, young boy-soldiers stopped us for inspection. With guns slung over their narrow shoulders, three walked into our motorhome as scrambled eggs and hash browns waited in the frying pan. Sniffing, marveling, they laughed saying, "*Desayuno, si?*" several times and left.

Clusters of doorless huts flanked by an occasional water tower was all I could see of the villages we passed. Some natives stood watching by the side of the road.

After breakfast I drove for an hour without seeing another vehicle. The jungle spread its ferns and grasses onto the shoulderless road, gutted with holes. I put a cassette in the tape deck and turned the volume up high, swerving to protect the tires from the worst ruts.

Rebecca screamed from the back of our twenty-nine foot

rig and came running to me.

"Stop! Didn't you see what happened, Mom? Someone may be hurt. A bus went off the road behind you!"

Lloyd stood at my side. "Let me handle it," he said. "Just pull off in the grass and wait."

He ran back a hundred yards. All I could see in the side view mirror was the white edge of a bus above the foliage. I envisioned the horror of people thrust on their sides, cut, broken, agonizing in contorted positions, hours away from medical care.

I wondered what a Mexican jail would be like and if my family would have to go home without me. I was responsible. Rebecca said the bus driver had honked as he tried to pass.

I wanted to hide. People were getting out of the bus. I could see them walking by the side of the road. The driver gesticulated wildly to my husband who spoke no Spanish. They walked up and down, in and out of my vision.

Finally, Lloyd returned. "The people are fine, shaken up is all." The driver had maneuvered safely into a ditch, keeping the bus upright. Instead of the side, I had been viewing the top of the bus! As we talked, it pulled up onto the road and drove off.

Quietly, I retreated to the back of the motorhome. My family didn't speak to me for hours, and then not about the accident. For years my negligence stayed buried. I knew no one in my family had forgotten but they never brought it up. The guilt gradually settled down in my memory.

I had some sympathy for my children as they got in accidents, but not enough. To me, "As long as you're okay nothing else really matters" was not true. I was sincerely grateful they were safe but I agonized over repair costs and hiked insurance premiums. Lloyd always kept an old car for our new drivers.

The children's accidents were mostly scrapes in parking lots. They were driving slowly, thinking they would clear the other vehicle and didn't. Our cars were rarely hurt; it was the nice cars they parked near that cost us.

"Rusty" was the "new driver vehicle" when one daughter came home from school on the first warm spring afternoon after she turned sixteen. A blond boy was waiting on a Moped by the side of the driveway. She slowed and rolled down the passenger window at the same time—talking, laughing and finally hitting the brick wall in the carport. She never took her eyes off the boy at any moment. I watched dumbfounded; I had to interrupt their conversation.

Stephen was our first child to own a car. For $100 he bought a '76 gold Dasher that overheated on trips over two miles. Riding with him took nerve—he carried plastic jugs of water in the back seat that he used to cool the engine at long stop lights. He was proud of his car. The gold color was not popular but it blended well with corroded metal. Stephen serviced it close by at Cash Saver since it needed the radiator and tires filled almost daily. On an afternoon when it needed gas too, the hose remained looped around the bumper. The nozzle flipped into the back window as he drove out. "Glass was still falling when Stephen leaped out, halting inches from my face," the gas station owner told me. "Indescribable...he was horrified. I've never seen a human expression like it."

"My car is ruined," Stephen moaned. Breakage under the hood was bearable but not a back window. Now it looked bad. Weeks later we were laughing, but that day we went out solemnly to mourn the results of his accident. In wet weather Stephen covered the opening with a picnic blanket.

After Stephen had died, I awoke on a Wednesday morning to thunder and heavy rain. I didn't want to get up or go driving. Andrew and John wanted a special breakfast. I fixed eggs with muffins and ate my wheat cereal beside them. I knew we had to be efficient. John's 7:45 A.M. piano lesson made him late for school if we didn't keep on schedule. His teacher lived across town; I never drove that far for any of the other children. We stepped off the back porch at 7:30 into water three inches deep. The street contained a river, turning into a lake at the corner.

We drove slowly. "Do you know about hydroplaning, John?" I asked.

"Have you ever seen it happen, Mom?" I had in Tennessee. A young man had spun off the road on his way to church. I had been behind him—the memory was vivid.

"I'll be back at exactly 8:15," I told John in front of his teacher's apartment. I tied my hood and snapped the green rain jacket, organizing an essay in my mind. Animated by facts on two trial cases I had reviewed with Lloyd that morning, I walked rapidly up the steep streets for maximum exercise and then hurried back to meet John.

We drove down to the main boulevard, past children walking to school. We were on schedule. Then I saw the woman running in the crosswalk, in her medical uniform and white shoes. I braked hard; I had no choice. I was propelled out of control toward the woman and the gutter. We swung around and struck solidly into the red curb. "Did I hit her, John?" I cried. I pulled open my door and ran around to the grass where she had landed. She held her knees up to her chest. There weren't even runs in her nylons.

"Did I hit you? Are you okay?" She said nothing. Her right eye was swelling, protruding like a golf ball out of her face. Her teeth were bloody. Another man joined us.

"Where do you hurt? Can we help you?" he asked.

"Some ice for my head," she responded. He looked at his insulated mug of hot coffee. Nurses in the medical building nearby had called the police. Blankets and coats appeared to cover her.

"I can't believe I hit her," I said.

Another woman told me, "You couldn't see her, I was right behind you. She was hidden by the other lane of traffic."

The police ushered me back into my car to fill out forms before the victim was taken in the ambulance. I found the registration in the glove compartment and my license in my purse, but there was no insurance card. Then I remembered Lloyd saying he was going to change companies. I had seen an insurance statement come in the mail that never got to my desk.

John went to a nearby phone to call a friend I was scheduled to pick up at 9:00 A.M. "What did you tell her John?" "I said we've had a little accident and you can't come." I liked his explanation even though it wasn't true.

I had cleared all of the woman's things off the street—her briefcase, her broken glass frames, one lens lying loose on the pavement, her lunch (a whole-wheat sandwich and a drink in a brown paper sack), and one shoe.

As I got out of my car to go with the investigating officer, I saw her other shoe. The toe was stuck under my left rear wheel like the movies in Driver's Education classes. I tried to pull the shoe from under the tire.

People were staring at me as I've stared at others at the scene of an accident. I felt naked and didn't care.

"What did I do wrong? What could I have done differently?" I quizzed the officer. "It was just her and the gutter, I had no place to go." "She had no place to go either," he said. "That's why we call it an accident." I knew he had used that phrase many times before. "Sign the citation. Anyone hitting a pedestrian in a crosswalk is cited. That's the law."

Lloyd came. We had a new insurance carrier; he would mail in the proof of coverage. "They towed my car to a paint and body shop. Back in our kitchen Lloyd said softly, "Anytime other cars are stopped at an intersection, you stop too, even if you don't see the pedestrian."

But I'd seen her in time to stop. If the car just hadn't slid!…then I was driving too fast for the weather conditions. I was quiet. I was guilty. I knew I would have said the same thing to one of our children. I could have gone to the bedroom and stayed in isolation; I considered it. Lloyd would have understood. But I was a different person than I had been years ago in Mexico.

I walked into Holy Cross Hospital on First South and found no lobby. I wandered into physical therapy rooms before finding my way through back doors to the emergency area. The receptionist was smiling. "I hit a woman with my car this morning," I said. "I want to stay until I know how she is and if there's something I can do." The nurse kept smiling. "The doctor's in X-ray. I think she's going to be all right. We'll keep you informed."

"She's an M.D.?" I asked. "Yes, she works here."

I sat down across from a woman with a new satin Broncos jacket around her shoulders; her head was down. Standing in the other corner was a man in a dark suit with an ID tag clipped to his pocket. White linoleum squares, durable floor mats, stark fluorescent lights—the waiting room was too ordinary for the agony occurring. I had observed this before, during the last surgery on Stephen.

A nurse from X-ray came to tell me the doctor was doing well. "She'll be down in a few minutes and then you can see her."

The man in a suit moved to the computer counter. The nurse phoned to make an appointment for his flu shot. "He'll be here as a guard for a few days," she explained to the scheduling nurse upstairs. He came over and sat by me, an undercover policeman on his first day back from a heart attack. "Someone called in a hostage threat," he said.

I went in to see the woman doctor. She asked me to stand on her left so she could see me out of her good eye. The other one was swollen shut and oozing blood. "I'm so sorry," I started. "You don't deserve this, walking to work with your briefcase and healthy lunch and then...to be hit."

"I know," she said as a tear ran down her bruised cheek. Resident doctors whom she supervised checked in on her; she was self-conscious. There was a cut on her toe and loosened teeth as well as her bulging eye, but no other injuries observed so far. She could be released that afternoon.

I took her glasses to be replaced and called her husband who was on a business trip in Nevada.

I told Emily, when she brought her children over for lunch, "I hit a woman! I hurt her. She did nothing wrong."

"I was an instrument of injustice," I told Martha. After school we took the new glasses to her. "Mom," Martha reasoned, "It's unjust for you too, you couldn't help sliding into her."

"But my actions caused her injury," I said. "I was at fault."

"When I got to school, the teacher read your note to the whole class," John told me as we fixed dinner. "At recess the kids were asking if you killed her."

"How far did we skid, John?"

"Across the whole intersection. It was slick like you worried about."

Martha went with me to deliver flowers to the woman that night. We got her prescription for pain medication filled. As we left, her friend asked, "How are you doing?"

A lull nearly disabled me. "Fine..." I said, it's her I'm concerned about."

"Well, I think there are at least two casualties in every accident," she replied.

I climbed in bed early. Rebecca had talked quietly with me on the phone sometime during the day. The shock of events had obscured the conversation until I lay there in the dark. "It was strange," I explained to her, "that when I felt like a guardian angel was cautioning me, that I wasn't able to avoid the accident."

"That's the way it usually works, isn't it?" she said. "We are comforted in a crisis but not removed. Aren't you glad to have felt something?"

The next day I worked in a frenzy, trying to compensate for the suffering I had caused. I knew grieving for Stephen had strengthened me. I was thankful the accident hadn't been worse; the woman was alive and could heal!

I took dinner to the doctor's house Friday evening. Her husband was back in town. "I've driven through crosswalks without noticing and been grateful no one was there to hit," he said. I don't think he knew the road was wet. It didn't matter anymore.

Saturday morning I lay in bed trying to imagine, in every part of my body, the pain that woman felt. "Under the Mosaic law," I said to Lloyd, "they might tie me to a whipping post and smash at my eye and mouth, cut my toe and beat me until I hurt like she does."

"Would that be justice?" he asked.

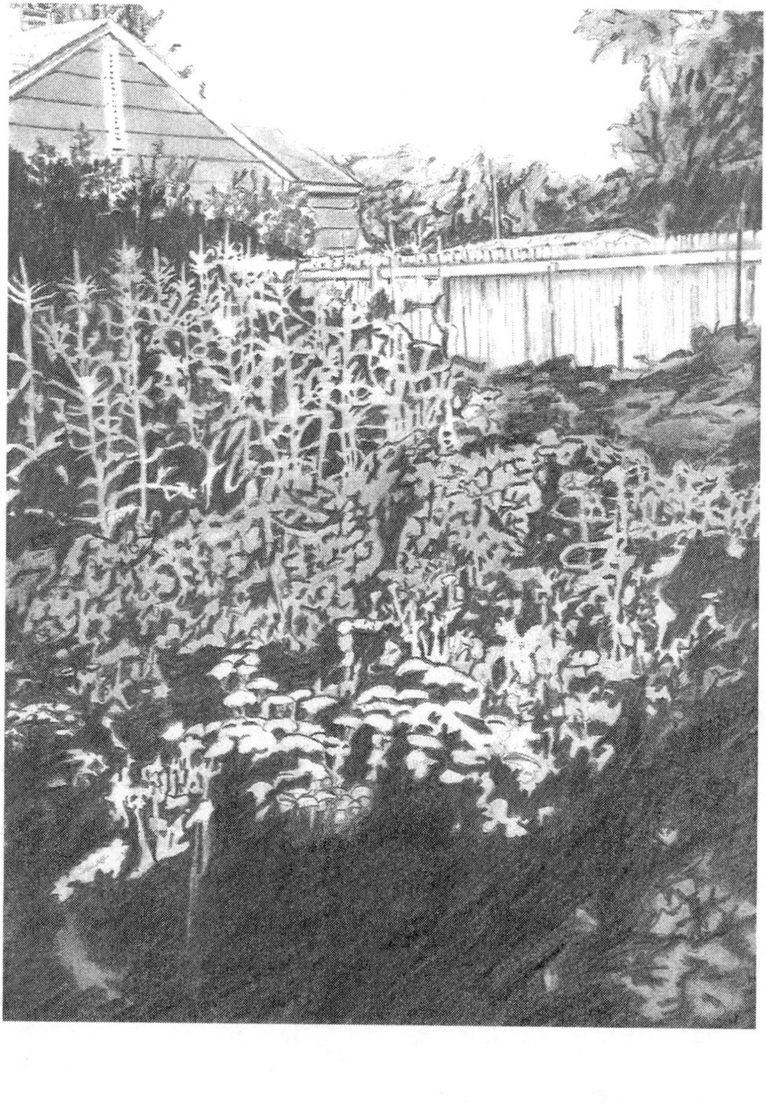

twelve

The Garden Plot

I like to dig in the dirt, trim bushes, plant seeds and pull weeds when they're big. I like to pick apples and break ears of corn off the stalks, not passionately as I used to, but because it's good to do. Lloyd would rather raise pigeons than tomatoes.

Twenty years ago our garden plot was grass and rose bushes. The Jewish doctor who owned the home before us had two hobbies, horticulture and rug tying.

He skillfully inserted a Jonathan graft into the Red Delicious apple tree so that both varieties of apples are harvested off the same tree. He planted all kinds of bulbs—lilies, hyacinths, and tulips. He trained grape vines to grow up the west fence and planted cherry trees between them and the house.

Two pine starts that he nurtured from seed on either side of the front sidewalk are gone. He tried to convey to us how precious they were, but Lloyd accidentally mowed them down the following spring. They were only as tall as the long grass.

The rose bushes were beautiful for the neighbors but we couldn't see them from the house. Pruning each year was tiresome.

One spring, after watering the lawn by the busy street, I went out with an edger and a shovel and cut the grass out in strips to form a nine by twelve foot rectangle. I loosened the ground with a digging fork and planted corn, tomatoes, beets, carrots and lettuce. I attached two hoses to a sprinkler and set it in the middle of the dirt. I watered and worried for a week and nothing happened. Days later when I had quit caring I noticed the corn, two inches tall, from my kitchen window and hustled the family outside to see. Our crop that summer was meager but my enthusiasm indomitable.

The next spring Lloyd hauled in horse manure with a truck. My brother-in-law from Vernal gave me a subscription to *Organic Gardening*. Our yield doubled and we began planning the demise of the roses.

We would make a garden encircled on three sides with sidewalk and a three-foot fence. The crops would be divided by rows of flowers to please the passers-by. Raspberries would line the tall fence on the fourth side, which would block the view of highway traffic from the house, and the apple tree would grow in the "orchard section" next to newly planted peach trees.

A tractor was brought in to clear the land; in hours the grass and rose bushes disappeared forever. The moist ground looked rich and fertile. The week the sidewalk was laid Lloyd brought in more manure and we planted corn. Rainbirds gyrated twice a day until the seeds germinated. Now I knew about nitrogen side dressings and applied them at six-week intervals. I sprayed the apple tree every ten days. Rebecca and I dug raspberry starts from a friend's garden and transported them in water and newspaper. Within four hours they were planted, never to go dry for the season. Powdered bone marrow strengthened the tomatoes, and when the blossoms opened we "set" them with spray so they would be guaranteed to produce.

The fourth spring was more exciting. We planted cold crops early. The peas went in as soon as the ground thawed, then broccoli, cauliflower and beets. Mr. Meadows, our 70-year-old neighbor, watched over the fence and asked questions. "Are you planting too early?"

"No, we're following the charts! It could never be too early for these crops."

I dreamed of a greenhouse where we could start seeds in January. Then I learned about a compost. All vegetable and fruit scraps, even eggshells must go with the grass clippings into a corner of the garden and be turned regularly. The corn grew higher than my head. To keep the children weeding, I hid wrapped candy in the dirt. We ate corn three meals a day during August and enough was left from the nubbins to freeze. A woman asked to use the dried cornstalks for decorating at a dinner dance. That fall we hauled the leaves from the front yard into the garden. The soil was too heavy— I wanted a soft loam.

"The compost is smelly," the children complained. I was delighted with an excuse to quit collecting peelings. Weekly, I helped the children empty the guinea pig droppings into the garden. Lloyd and I decided to eliminate the truck-load of manure that carried weed seeds. The leaves didn't fully decompose in the winter but we plowed them under and planted on top. "We're going to streamline this year," I announced. "The crops that get slugs are out. We'll specialize." Lloyd plowed up the asparagus.

"Plant the rows two feet apart," my brother-in-law said.

"Weed with your plow." My husband quit plowing after planting that year. It was the spring he had over-fertilized the tomato starts, which killed every one.

Lloyd built a pigeon loft, filling the coops with Helmets, Rollers, Tumblers and a pair of Homers. He had raised pigeons as a youth and gave the children their own birds, which they watched grow from balls of down to cocks and hens. The pigeons strutted down their arms and fluttered to the ground when dropped in mid air. The pigeon droppings went into the garden.

Lloyd taught the children to check for infertile eggs with a flashlight, band the squabs' legs, and fill the feed troughs, but when winter came he was the only one who walked through the snow to break the ice in the drinking vessels. Dust and an occasional fluff feather clung to his dark suit all the way to the office.

"If you want the pigeons, you've got to help," Lloyd said to the children. There were sixty-two birds the winter after Oreo and Petro got ribbons at the State Fair. I never offered to help. Birds were too jittery—they scared me.

"Why don't we grow peas anymore?" the children asked. I had decided to limit my time in the garden from May 15 to the first freeze in the fall. "I've got to save my strength to harvest," I told Lloyd.

A neighbor moved in from California and proposed sharecropping. "I've noticed how well your weeds grow," he said. "I think you have good soil." He planted carrots and beets. I planted corn, since I was the expert on it, and we both planted tomatoes. The corn never reached my shoulders that year. The California man told me I had too much morning glory and that his wife wanted him working in their garden.

A third of the pigeons died the night a stray one-eyed cat got into the loft. Lloyd gave the rest of the birds away except for the white homing pigeons he couldn't catch. They revisited every few weeks, lighting on the telephone wires in the backyard until the cold came again. Lloyd turned the loft back into a storage shed. "It's not the messy chores I miss, it's the process," he said. "I liked watching the hens brood over their eggs…I liked feeding a Homer out of my hand."

Then came the year of the "pygmy corn." The children helped plant as usual and quit. I wasn't sure I liked the garden enough to perpetuate it myself. I added nitrogen and the corn didn't grow as high as my waist. I couldn't abandon the garden; it lay exposed on a busy boulevard—the tomatoes were doing well. I tried to weed early in the morning when people wouldn't patronize me but the joggers were out at all hours.

"Nice garden," they'd yell. "It must take a lot of effort." They went so fast I didn't have time to explain, but what I would explain I hadn't figured out. The walkers said, "It's been a hard year for our garden, too."

"Why can't someone ignore my one crop failure?" I asked Lloyd at night.

"I can't believe our garden is doing so poorly!" I said at breakfast. "Remember when the corn was as high as my head?" Stephen turned his clear blue gaze intently on me. "Mom, we've never really been known for our garden."

The truth! There it was. I could deal with it. I took a soil sample down to the garden shop—it had no nutrients. How simple and easily solved. I copied down the recipe for super soil from the consultant at the counter; sphagnum peat, pellet iron, soil sulfur, Borax, 10-10-10-8 fertilizer, sand and more Epsom salts.

The next year I would show our children how good the garden used to be. Our garden had patterned my adult life. Early success preceded complex challenges. I was not willing to give up. I saved the recipe all winter on top of my desk and in late April purchased 200 pounds of soil additives. We calendared a date in the middle of May—everyone was going to help. Stephen drove in from his house project. Bag after bag was torn open and spread across the ground. Dust fogged the air. We dug it under immediately with shovels and later

Lloyd plowed.

We planted only corn, tomatoes and squash. Each member of the family was responsible for weeding two rows all summer. We canned 100 quarts of tomatoes and ate the corn and squash.

I put our phone number on a sign in the dirt the spring Stephen died. "Interested in sharing our garden?" it said. No one called. I covered the morning glory with black plastic. I planted perennial flowers and tomatoes. I talked to the soil like I had seen Lloyd talk to his pigeons, oblivious to passersby. The earth was gentle and indulgent, subservient to my wants like Pliny had discovered centuries ago. I started to heal by cooperating with nature to perpetuate life. The pumpkins never turned orange but the zucchini and chrysanthemums thrived.

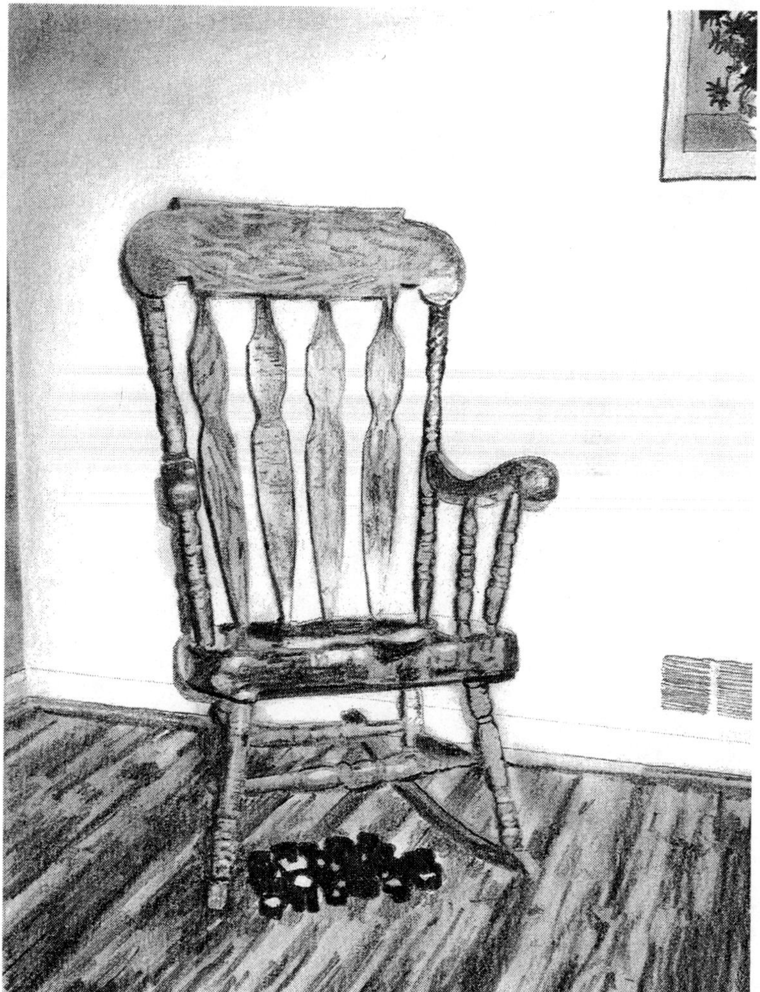

thirteen

Chocolates

Just like I had grand illusions, my parents thought they could teach me to like work by gardening. Their move from New York to Utah in the early 1950s enhanced that opportunity. My father purchased two lots—one with a house and one to cultivate vegetables. In addition, he planted a rock garden along a bank next to the irrigation ditch. I weeded. With hand clippers I trimmed the grass that bordered the garden and also all around the house. To expand our skills, Father bought a hundred chicks for Easter. We tended them in an incubator and helped build a coop across the stream where they grew all summer. The weekend before school started we hauled them, fat and squawking, to the slaughter house. The next year he gave us two rabbits, insisted we butcher them at the end of the season and eat them. I was the only one in my family with braces on my teeth. I had an excuse for not eating rabbit and I used it for deer meat, too, that we cut and packaged after my father and brothers returned from a fall hunt.

When I was young I worked when I was told. I watched a brother get disciplined for failing to thin the beets and a sister for reading while she vacuumed the same spot of carpet over and over.

I didn't like to work until I got paid for it. At age eleven I started babysitting and my earnings accumulated in a tin refrigerator bank. Eventually Father went with me to open an account at a Savings and Loan where the interest rates were highest even though he told me he didn't trust the institution. "I will personally insure your money," he promised.

Money motivated me to work beyond my assigned tasks at home. I waitressed at the Hot Shoppes and served meals at a hospital. I filed insurance statements for months and hated every minute, but I stuck it out because I could see the lucrative reward.

Stephen learned to work like I did. He was no more eager to clean his room or do Saturday jobs than the other children. It was the thought of money in his hand that was powerful, not just a pittance for allowance but multiples of what another teenage boy earned mowing our grass.

His lawn care partnership took off and saturated the neighborhood. Then it was easy for him to find other yard work. He was strong and rich and in demand. "You're the only one who can help me finish harvesting the cherries, Stephen," I said, "and I'll pay you." He climbed the thirty-foot trees with a hand saw and cut off the upper limbs so the younger children could pick the laden branches. He didn't take time to eat lunch that day before heading to a job shoveling dirt. I was proud of Stephen. I never imagined I would have a twelve-year-old son who could outwork me.

Stephen was tired of his yard business the fall we bought

the Mill, primed for a change. He had learned to like the results of his work even without pay. When spring came he was broke and wanted to resume the lawn jobs. "You burned out last year, Stephen. Consider a change."

"It's good money, good exercise. I can stand it with my Walkman."

By July he was miserable. We divided each week; the first three days were spent building at the Mill and the next three keeping up in Salt Lake. All enthusiasm for work left him each time we returned. By September I was fielding phone calls from his customers. We both hoped it would turn cold so grass would stop growing.

When Stephen made up his mind to go to Hawaii in the winter, a neighbor who had lived there came to visit. "I've watched people picking pineapples, Stephen. It's peon's work—mindless, back-breaking, dirty labor."

"I know how to do that," he said.

"It doesn't sound bad," Lloyd told me when we were alone. "Hard physical labor did more than anything to persuade me to get an education."

The letters from Stephen in Hawaii came regularly.

"The work is a lot harder here than I imagined. Mike, I don't mean to discourage you but it's not easy. Right now my wrist and lower arms ache like crazy. You also get scratches all the way up your arms and all over your chest. By the time the day is over my shirt and Levis are literally wet from sweating."

The next week he wrote, "Although the work is hard I enjoy it. At least when you go to bed at night you know you've done something. The people here are not cute little boy scouts. Many used to have earrings [they don't allow them here], some are trendies and some used to be drug dealers and some are just good kids but you don't have to worry about anyone doing anything wrong or else they are sent home."

The third week he was "getting used to the work as a fact of life."

And the fourth week it rained. He only worked 36 hours instead of the previous 49. "It depresses me not to be able to work. I want the money and I don't like sitting around. There's so much time to think that you seem to go crazy sometimes and wish you had to work. Yesterday the nurse gave me penicillin and a tetanus shot for my swollen glands. Today my neck hurts more. At least I can still work, I just can't swallow much."

Two months from the time he arrived in Hawaii, he decided to break his contract and come home.

"Please stay, Stephen. You made a commitment. You'll lose your profit if you return early," I wrote back.

I was panicky. It appeared to me that nothing could motivate Stephen to stay. He was developing a pattern of burn out. Finishing the job was my inherited measure of success in preparing a child for a productive life. I couldn't understand Stephen's reversal. He had learned to work earlier than the other children and with much less effort on my part.

I thought this crisis in Stephen's life related to boredom. As a young mother I imagined I would go crazy doing cleaning and laundry. Lloyd joined a tape club for me so I could hear books on cassette while I worked. I listened until I had enough in my mind to think about something other than what I was doing. I knew I could never endure working in a pineapple field.

Lloyd wrote to Stephen about Eric Hoffer. "He works as a longshoreman in New York—loading cargo into ships. It is rough manual labor spent with people of meager education. But when he's off work he buries himself in reading and writing. He's an author and philosopher."

After a 6:00 A.M. to 3:00 P.M. workday picking pineapples, Stephen started to spend the rest of his time studying. In a week he had finished his English credit and a term of math.

"This might not have been a good idea for me to come here," he wrote, "but it also might have. Anyway, being the bullhead that I am I'm going to try to stay." He finished a course on American government, novels, and started one on short stories. I eliminated boredom as a cause of his restlessness. "I hope I didn't scare you with my last letter," Stephen wrote. "I guess I get awfully depressed to hear from my friends and what a good time they are having and how they wish I were there."

I continued to explore from my own experience why Stephen was restive. Maybe he was having difficulty adjusting to the persistent rhythm of life. That had been hard for me to bear when he was a child. "Life is too hard," I had told my mother. "We don't have enough strength after we finish our work for any fun," I told Lloyd. And Lloyd just kept working. I heard people talk about workaholics and I wondered if that description fit my husband. I would never accuse him of it because he provided well. He knew the importance of vacations with our family and enjoyed them—after a two-day headache. We had been married almost 20 years and he never lost motivation. His diligence sometimes frustrated me. I was content to leave a dirty kitchen at night rationalizing that to finish the job was impossible. Lloyd had to clean it up. "But you don't want to wake up to a mess do you?" he asked.

And then I learned his secret. I was recovering from infectious mononucleosis at age 38. I had spent a month in bed. Lloyd contracted it from me and kept working. One Saturday morning he couldn't get out of bed. He lay there quiet with his eyes open and didn't move.

"Are you okay?" I asked. He didn't look over. He didn't say anything. "Why do you have to work so hard? You need to take a week off. You need rest as much as I do."

No response. I knew why he didn't take time off. He was in the middle of critical cases. We had children in college. It was more than absorbing work that kept him going. It was survival.

Twenty minutes later he said, "I'm scared."

His answer washed over me like cold water. I was nineteen when I married him; he was nine years older. He had worked, before I met him, up from nothing. He knew the embarrassment of no pocket change as a boy and had progressed to a practicing lawyer.

"I learned in law school," he said, "that I wasn't brilliant like some of my peers, but that if I worked harder, if I was always prepared, I could compete."

I stayed quiet for a long time. I had never linked work to fear. I knew about fear; I met it as a young child. I believe it is unavoidable and universal but I never imagined I could share my life with someone and not share his fear. I thought about a journalist's recent account of a young man in Beirut, pulled from bed and the arms of his wife by militants. Suddenly, he had stood outside on the street in terror. His wife at the doorway, wrapped in a blanket, could do nothing. He was alone. That is the nature of deepest fear.

"How did you feel all those years I resisted your overtime at the office?" I braced myself for his answer.

We had a month reprieve before Stephen was sent home. His desire to return was a more complex issue than finishing the job. Eric Hoffer described what Stephen was experiencing as the frustration of misfits, the temporary variety, "people who have not found their place in life but still hope to find it. They are restless, dissatisfied and haunted by the fear that their best years will be wasted before they reach their goal."

At age five I was plagued by fear. I had crawled under my sister's full-size bed in Flushing. A heavy man had been a guest overnight in that bed some time before and had broken the wooden frame. A suitcase held the box springs up and hid me from view. I often stayed in this place. My sister had the prettiest room, blue and yellow with white starched curtains, and it was private. I kept a collection under her bed. Every time we had guests for Sunday dinner my mother served each of us a chocolate. I never ate mine but carried it upstairs to enlarge my collection. I arranged the chocolates in their fluted paper cups under my sister's rocking chair; it acted as a kind of frame. I smelled each one and then pushed them carefully back, far under in the middle where the bag would protect my chocolates from the vacuum.

Father had been yelling for me. I knew he already missed his train from Long Island into the city and that he was still in his pajamas. After another half hour he stopped looking for me to dress. I took my chocolates out. I was alone. Everyone else had gone to school but my preschooler brother who was downstairs with mother.

I was scared. The new coat my parents bought for me had two sets of buttons, a zipper, and a hood that tied. Mother made sure it was all done up tightly before I walked to Public School 107. When the bell rang in the playground I had started to be afraid. We marched in single file up two flights of stairs and were expected to take our coats off immediately and be ready to say the pledge of allegiance in unison with the loudspeaker broadcast. I couldn't do it. I couldn't get all those buttons undone and the zipper too. The day before I had been hurrying so fast the tie knotted and my teacher yelled at me.

I couldn't return to school. My father was shaving, soon to resume his search. I started to eat my chocolates. I ate every one, all twenty-eight.

Fear can be rash. It affects people in unpredictable ways. It may have nothing or everything to do with wanting to work and finishing jobs. The same haunting that motivated my husband for a lifetime erratically immobilized my son.

I was able to outlive the anxieties of my youth. Once I had finished college, I no longer suffered from diarrhea the morning of an exam. After I married, I didn't acquire rashes over my chest and neck before dances. My fears had been in anticipation of situations that no longer existed. As I raised our children I developed new concerns. I was afraid I would be incompetent when I finally had time for more education and civic service. I feared collapse. Many nights I was tempted to take the Cheyenne Exit away from Salt Lake City, or the Savannah Exit away from Nashville—interested in going anywhere except home to my responsibilities. But the fear of neglecting my children was the strongest of all, and I continued to work hard.

When John began school I returned to the university. I measured my progress in dealing with anxiety. I had improved. I worked more diligently and worried less. But I still ate too much during finals week—my enduring reaction to all fear. Concern for my children's future was finally under control. I had ceased to dread that one of them would fail because it was fruitless. That kind of worry did no good.

Then I encountered my worst fear—one so deep I had never considered it before. Nothing softened the blow. The fact that I did not anticipate Stephen's death took me past a whole stage of reactions. I did not eat chocolates after he died. I did not eat, until Lloyd encouraged me a day later. My worst fear had come and gone without my participation. After days of numbness I comprehended that the only thing left to decide was whether I stay immobilized with his death or use it as motivation to strengthen my husband and our devastated children. Fear, the type that presages tragedy, had lost its power over me. It had pushed too far. I would grieve as deeply at future tragedy but not be clutched by fear.

fourteen

The Sack

The leftovers were in the refrigerator and the dishwasher started. Rebecca was anxious to see what Halloween costumes would fit her daughter before going home. We walked together down the back stairs, past the pantry, to the costume closet. Emily came after with her three-year-old.

Outfits draped on hangers—a jeweled fuchsia gown, a blue-striped clown suit, hospital fatigues, a crocodile jumpsuit. Labeled in black plastic bags were costume accessories— shoes, hats, wigs and masks, sheets, and finally, a bag marked "miscellaneous."

Rebecca wanted the leopard costume for her child who didn't care what she wore. Emily felt sure her little girl wanted to be a witch but as we opened the black sacks one at a time her daughter changed her mind. "Maybe I will be a cat. Maybe I will be a ghost." One sack was different, made of fabric. "It's heavy as a corpse," I said, dragging it from the back of the closet. It was not labeled so I set it aside.

At the bottom of the "misc." bag, we found the thin, lace-trimmed witch dress originally worn by my oldest sister. I held it up for my granddaughter to inspect but Emily was the one most interested. The three-year-olds played on storage boxes and a blue wooden rocking horse.

We stuffed the bags back into the closet, coming again to the fabric one. "Oh, I hope this isn't Stephen's," I said, feeling the weight again and vaguely remembering. I took a loose-leaf out. "No, it's Andrew's writing, isn't it?"

The first week at school after the summer of grieving, a junior high school teacher called Andrew "Stephen" five times. "Well, you look just like Stephen did eight years ago," she explained. At back-to-school night I asked her to be cautious; I didn't know better.

The loose-leaf in my hand had unsent letters, one to Andrew. "Andrew, I think we are quite alike physically. When I was your age, I was really small. I still am. My advice is to forget it, so if you grow, it will be a nice surprise."

The next loose-leaf was white, organized with tabs by category: sports, professions, building supplies. Pages of lists included the equipment needed and opposite, beside a ruled line, was highlighted, "Bright Side"—followed by things to invent or market in the field. The loose-leaf was full.

Rebecca and Emily sat crouched on the floor beside the freezer. They had no intention of leaving. I reached again into the sack and found two heavy-metal guitar magazines and one on speed picking. Brochures on his new keyboard were still in a brown envelope. Three worn pocket folders of guitar music spilled out; he never played a group of Christmas carols for us that he had obviously learned.

I heard my daughters' husbands pacing with the babies in

the kitchen above. New colored folders were separately labeled—Song Ideas and Lyrics, Weekly Goal Book, Words for the Wise, Music Log, and What I Think About Things.

There was too much. I handed the folders to Rebecca. "I want to read them," she said. "I didn't know Stephen that well."

The next item was a journal started when Stephen left to work in Hawaii. One hundred and ten pages were written during the fall of 1990. The last entry was November 18. "I kinda fell apart today. I ate too much. My goal backfired on me—it was too much of an extreme." He added bread to his Tofu and fruit diet.

"Stephen recorded more in two years than I have in my life," said Rebecca, our English graduate student. We searched to find the other journal. The entries in it were shorter and less frequent. They took him through his fears of breakdown and the tedious job he had in Arizona when he could barely hold on.

Books came out of the sack, *Celebrate the Temporary,* and *One Hundred and One Famous Poems,* plus two sets of motivation cassettes.

A packet of letters received after he left home for the first time at age sixteen lightened the bag immensely. The grandchildren were fighting over the wooden horse. Emily hushed them quickly.

Only a file box remained. Stephen had copied famous quotes on wealth, discipline, and diet, and augmented then with his own lists of beliefs. "I believe I can think what and how I want. Every human is equal. I believe you should try your hardest every day. I want to be me, Stephen Lloyd Poelman."

I left the folders and box on the floor next to the sack and added the journals to Rebecca's pile.

Emily wanted to read the findings too. I knew she wanted to share in everything but I worried about her tendencies toward depression. "Make sure you're strong enough," I encouraged. The sack was empty.

After Stephen had sold the house, he marketed raspberries while the weather stayed good, avoiding his typical burnout by reading and writing on the job. When the rest of the children had started school, Lloyd loaned Stephen *Personal Power*, a series of motivation cassettes. Stephen set goals for himself in thirteen categories—physical, financial, nutritional, educational, moral, emotional, charitable... subdivided into lists totaling seven pages.

He wrote in his journal, "My life will be like going down a river. I will have the current going for me but because I want more success, I'm going to paddle as fast as I can. For years, I was trying to paddle upstream—my efforts were canceled out by the flow. I want motivation and the natural laws on my side and I'll be unstoppable."

Over Labor Day, Stephen had quit playing the bass guitar for Innocent Jubilation, a rock band that he joined in the summer. After he announced his decision the other musicians kept calling and coming to the door. Stephen shut himself in his room while we were at the Mill. "I didn't want to be slowed down anymore with their problems," he said. Stephen started practicing on his own two hours a day.

Every morning Stephen got up at 6:00 A.M. to read and type onto the computer. "I want to change this world." Stephen wrote. "I will gradually increase my self control to where I can feel any way I want at any given time. I want to write three novels this year."

On school days, Stephen came into the kitchen at 6:30 A.M. to fix Martha breakfast and make her a sack lunch. "I'm going to help her lose weight and she can't do it missing meals," he said. He put Post-it notes next to her sandwich. "Enjoy this—prepare for a light dinner." He persuaded me to eliminate oil in homemade bread and halve the shortening in cookies. He was as disciplined as he wanted others to be. "I ate Malt-o-Meal and cantaloupe for breakfast, salad and cantaloupe for lunch and an apple and cantaloupe for dinner," he wrote. "As far as eating habits, today was awesome."

Stephen had started sewing lessons—he evaluated the pros and cons. "It expands your horizons, is a fun hobby with business potential, makes character, saves money, will give me something to do during winter, is a show field, [if you're good], but, people think you're weird and you might poke yourself...there are no obvious drawbacks!" He bought sporty knit fabric in a variety of colors and made designer shirts. Mike and Martha borrowed them to wear to school.

On a rainy day when his pick-up truck was in the shop, I drove Stephen to his guitar lesson. "My teacher makes his living off music," Stephen said, "not just teaching—he plays other jobs. He could go on tour if he wanted."

Stephen bought a four track recorder, a microphone and a drum machine. "I want to be a creator, not just a liver. I will no longer practice other people's music. If I want to play something neat, I'll have to make it up. I will have an album out in a year."

He mowed lawns during breaks, worked at the Wool and Leather Shop in the evenings and averaged six to eight hours on his music. He wrote down a daily schedule after the first hard frost.

6:00-6:45	type on computer—something besides music
7:00-8:00	guitar
8:00-8:30	breakfast
8:45-9:45	lyrics
10:00-10:30	vocals
10:30-11:30	drum machine
11:45-12:30	keyboard
Lunch—socialize	
1:30-2:30	guitar
2:30-3:00	bass
3:15-3:45	drum machine
4:00-4:30	lyrics

4:30-5:00	vocals
5:00-6:30	exercise
6:30-7:30	guitar
7:30-10:00	ABSOLUTELY ANYTHING YOU WANT (one thing charitable)
10:00-10:30	harmonica
10:30	journal, observe

We talked at the kitchen table during lunch and on the evenings when he was off work. During fall quarter, I studied Spanish at the kitchen table with a glass of water and a pile of sugar-free Sorbees. I liked talking with Stephen.

"How can you stand getting pushed into doing lots of stuff you don't want to?" Stephen asked me. "If I went back to the 'U', I would have to take classes that don't interest me. I want to decide every aspect of my life."

"I decided some things," I said, "but after that, a lot of my life just happened. I've ended up content with experience I didn't know I wanted."

He listened. He leaned forward onto the white formica table. "I want to make things happen. I really think if I work hard enough I can. 'Everything in nature, even dust and feathers go by law and not by luck,' that's from Emerson. What he sows, he reaps. Do you believe it?" he asked.

"I need to take life seriously," he wrote, "so when people are coming home from their missions I'm not left behind. That's why I'm glad I'm not drinking and having too much of a social life lately. Either are the missionaries and if I can train myself to have the restraints they have, I'll have great control."

Stephen took a week off to go to the Mill to concentrate on music full time. He practiced eight hours Sunday through Thursday and then made cupcakes to go with his dinner. It was Halloween.

"The cupcakes were a waste of time, energy and ruined my health for the day, but I made a breakthrough. I figured out that you pick a good topic, make a catchy chorus, and then do the verses—you make the music to enhance the lyrics."

They're strange people out there
A fat lady who thinks she's skinny
Rich man without enough money

People who won't eat red meat
Starving people with nothing to eat

The killer, the doctor,
the preacher, the thief
famous people we'd all
kill to meet. Gangs and
drunks all out on the street.

Stephen came home the next day.
"Did you see all those smashed pumpkins on the street," he said. "It's a waste." He was watching me make pumpkin pie from our Jack-o'-lanterns.

"If I hadn't brought my pumpkins in last night, they would have been wasted too."

"I never used to touch yours," Stephen said. I turned from the sink piled with cooked peelings to look at his face. He laughed. "For once, I'm innocent. No one but you cares about their pumpkins after Halloween." He circled the kitchen table quizzing me on the other ingredients, figuring he could make a pie from discarded pumpkins for less than a dollar and market it for $7.

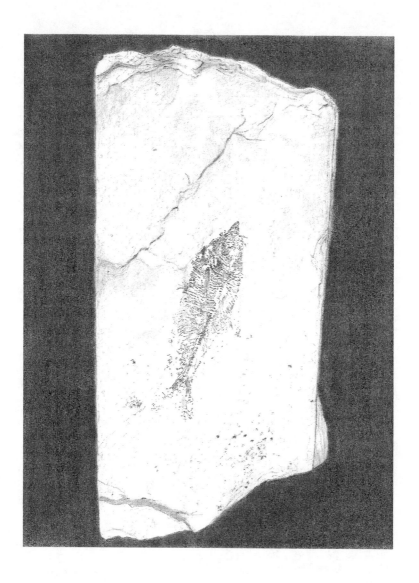

fifteen

Ditto

During the rush hour a man appeared by our home holding a sign. "Work For Food," it said, "I Have A Wife And Three Children." I found Stephen loading a sack with canned stew, oranges, a loaf of bread and packages of Twinkies.

"Sure, go ahead and take it to him." I felt guilty knowing I wouldn't have contributed on my own. A few minutes later Stephen returned with the sack.

"The guy didn't want the food," Stephen said. "He didn't want to have to carry it. He just wanted money." Stephen was disconcerted; the man drained contributions we knew should go to the genuine poor. "That guy will probably make more money in an hour than I made all day."

Stephen fostered a conviction of equality. "Why should some people have so much more than others," he said. "They don't deserve it…they're no better." That attitude was his justification for stealing before the "rush" of the act took over. I am not sure what prompted the change from idealism to lawlessness but I think it was affected by the day a stray golf ball landed in his path. Instead of pocketing and selling it as he had done for years, he decided to throw it back across the street onto the fairway. He did not wait to see the ball drop short and bounce into southbound traffic. The woman whose windshield was shattered chased him down.

"It isn't fair!" Stephen was furious. "The ball could have broken a windshield when it hit the highway the first time. That lady never would have caught the golfer." He perceived justice as "rendering to every man his due." When Stephen received an extra dose of injustice he struck out to even things up again.

For his English class he wrote an essay on revenge. "If someone toilet papers my house with three rolls I will get him back with ten rolls and a dozen eggs. If someone picks on my sister I will gather all the dung from the dog run into a paper sack and I will take it to his house and burn it on his front porch."

When Stephen left to work in Hawaii I thought we were ahead of his friends' parents, who didn't know the scope of their sons' daring. I later learned we were years behind. I discovered Stephen's motivation for departure and a job that required physical strength. He wrote, "I left because I thought I hated my parents and that they weren't satisfied until I found out that I'm not satisfied with myself…I've done a lot of things wrong…My goal is to get into incredible shape and be very muscley. My friends are all strong and I want to be very much like them. I want to be a fighter. When I get home I want to be tough and beat up people if I want."

The time we spent apart was advantageous. After he had been in Hawaii a month, I answered the doorbell late on a

Friday. Two policemen asked for him and I was thrilled to inform them he was far away from any illegal act that was committed that night. He was safe, we were safe for the present. Distance opened up communication. Rebecca wrote a six-page letter to him. "I might be wrong about this [tell me if I am] but mom and dad seem to think that just lately, as in the couple of months before you left, you were going off the wall. They seem to think that only recently have there been major troubles. But it appears to me that only lately things came to the surface—but they existed underneath for a longer time. In the past, you'd been saying 'yes' but meaning 'no' and just lately you've been saying 'no' when you mean it. There's some good in the lately part because it's more honest, but it also means more waves…Maybe when you come home you won't feel so explosive and can figure out how to be yourself without going overboard."

Stephen wrote in his journal about Rebecca's letter. "She changed a lot of my feelings. She told me some of mom and dad's faults. They are not big faults but they helped me know that not everything is my fault but most of it is. They're extremists, they look at everything and judge it as either bad or good and aren't afraid to say just what they think about what I've been doing. If I acted like they did then they'd be in for a big surprise…"

I did not appreciate my children's criticism then like I do now. I was a fragile parent, as inexperienced in directing my son as he was in being one.

Rebecca explained to Stephen, "I like mom and dad's dedication and enthusiasm in parenting but some of their 'style' is hard for me. I have a confusing time sometimes talking to them—because they're often asking me 'Isn't this fun!' 'Don't you like this!' or 'Hasn't this been one of the best times we've had together!' and I don't want to crush them by saying 'No—it wasn't the best' but I also don't like to be dishonest and say 'Yes' when I don't really mean it."

What irritated our daughter has always bothered me.

When someone declares their response to a scene I am still evaluating, I feel manipulated. "Let me think for myself," I say. But I had no capacity to see the defect I imposed on my children. I was too busy being in charge.

Deep feelings were generated by our children. "I can tell that I have a strong attachment to mom and dad," Rebecca wrote, "because when I hear other people talk about them, I'm either proud if they're talked nicely about or very defensive if they're talked about in a bad way. But, I'm also very rough on them [not to their face, but in my mind.] When I don't like something they do, I can't toss their 'faults' off as easily as I can overlook the faults of other people. It's intense because I love them strongly plus I dislike some of their behaviors strongly."

Rebecca had recently married and moved away. She acknowledged Stephen's diverse nature as she felt her own developing. Stephen ventilated his frustrations in his journal. "Mom and dad look at how they were when they were young and think I should be that way so I can be successful too. The truth is what they lived on as kids I would die on. I guess parents for some reason want their kids to grow up just like them and that can happen 'cause some kids are like their parents. This kid is not. It's hard to believe that me, coming half from dad and half from mom could be so unlike either of them. It's like mom and dad are two negatives and when I was made, I became a positive."

I am not sure that the differences between us and our children were attributable solely to styles. As a teenager I could have written the same letter Rebecca wrote to her sibling, about my parents. And ever since I was Rebecca's age my goal for when I became a parent had been unchanged—the sooner my child would feel like a close friend to me the better. I planned to bypass the typical pattern. But I couldn't.

After our first child was born I tried to comprehend my new identity. I continued school for another year at the university. One morning I was rushing to take my baby to a woman in the neighborhood and still get to an 8:50 A.M. class on time. We lived in an apartment up four flights of stairs from the street. I tripped, fell and kept her up, landing seated on the top of the second flight. I looked inches away into her face peeking out from a furry hood. My helpless daughter was just like I had been twenty years earlier.

As she grew I didn't get along with her. She was head-strong and impulsive; our similarities irritated. I worried about not liking my oldest daughter very much. My attitude changed when she turned twelve. She was the violinist I had wanted to be. I respected her in time for the teen years, and learned from her.

In Tennessee I decided to start jogging. I had finished having children and craved being fit for the rest of my life. In the recovery room after John's birth, I did sit-ups. I told Lloyd to stand watch for nurses. "Can't you take a day off?" he asked. I wasn't trying to be heroic; I imagined myself gliding for miles past white fences and horses.

Six weeks later I jogged down Long Valley Road and up High Lea for the first time. Liz and I had planned to go together but I was ready first and wanted to warm up, assuming she would catch me. She stood watching in the driveway as I rounded the bend toward home.

"Good things are happening," I said. "I itch like crazy."

"You could go faster, Mom."

"No, I've got to work up gradually."

"It won't take more energy. Just move horizontally."

What kind of a comment is that? I thought. I'm running! Liz jogged beside me.

"Push forward," she said. "You should be able to see your legs in front of you."

The new movement felt strange; high school Pep Club training was obsolete. "Now level out," she said, "not so jerky." My speed doubled. All the children were waiting outside as we returned.

"You did a great job, Liz," Rebecca said. Then she turned to me. "Mom, you look tons better."

I had teenage children who were my friends. I had reached my goal only to have it slip away for a night with one child, or a few weeks with another, or years. "It's a stage," I said. But I had to delineate whether it was their stage to be endured or mine. I knew that a relationship of inequality was transitory. The enduring friendship between my children and me would grow to exist between us as equals.

The spring Emily moved back from California she gave me a note. I thrived on her new openness. "Please understand this is a hard letter to write. Thank you for somewhat understanding me. I know you try. I try to understand you. Just know that I love you and dad. It's just so hard to show it because of all the things we have been through."

Stephen grew beyond belligerency with his focus on equality intact. Instead of equal rights or possessions, he championed equality of worth. He seemed to believe in Plato's definition that "men are made, all, of the same earth by the same creator. As dear to God is the poor peasant as the mighty prince."

One summer evening after work he walked through the house to the patio and surveyed the situation. Andrew had invited boyfriends for a swim. Mike, six years older than Andrew, was there too, with a friend. The bigger boys dominated the pool from a rubber raft, bullying every attempt by the others to dive or do anything but duck away. Stephen changed clothes and walked out as Andrew and his friends were starting to leave the pool. He capsized the raft, dunking Mike and his friend until they left. Stephen played water polo with the twelve-year-olds for the next hour.

When Stephen started college he had a more consistent grip on fair mindedness than I. He sought diverse relationships. I did too, but whenever I had the attitude "Well, you know how so and so is," he would flatten me out.

"That's a judgment, Mom. Maybe they aren't that way."

I wasn't offended. A few years earlier I probably would have been, and he wouldn't have dared tell me the truth about myself until we were friends.

Just before Liz married, we were camping on a Mexican beach at La Salina. I had completed three quarters of Spanish. I wanted to improve my speech and comprehension as much as possible. Reentering the campground the second day, after a trip to the fish market, I rolled down my window to talk to the Mexican attendant. Paid—we've already paid is what I wanted to say. I thought the verb was *pegar*. "*Antes de...yo...pegar.*"

"Mom," Liz was interjecting from the back seat. "The verb is *pagar*."

I could hear she was trying to correct me. I remembered I wasn't using the past tense—that must be the problem. "Don't help me," I said. "I can do this."

"*Pega...pegamento.*"

The man waved his hand in disgust. Liz was quiet. "What did Mom say?" Mike asked.

"She told him to 'hit glue' and he's still letting us in."

I had progressed from being innocent to naive to just dumb. My children liked me more. There was no inequality between us and when I domineered they only had to recall the times of my humiliation so we could laugh together.

Stephen refined my conscience even though he wasn't without his own biases. Weeks before he died he told me, "I have no more anger but there's still one guy who needs a punch in the nose for his own good. One clean blow, Mom." He was smiling. The intensity he had felt to enforce others' behavior had subsided.

I was still judgmental. I wanted Stephen to help me change. We developed an unspoken code. His cautioning words became a glance, then a "here we go again" aspect, so familiar that I read "ditto" in his eyes.

It was months after he died before I could begin to miss him constructively. I went into a do-it-yourself framing shop to price a shadow box.

"You will probably need us to do the work for you," the woman said. "The procedure is quite complicated...you'll have to buy..."

I could hear the woman talking but my mind was recalling the young man who had waited on me years before. Instead of being irritated, he had smiled. "You can do a shadow box in two hours. I'll help you," he had said. "That's the most incredible fossil I have ever seen."

I had been framing a rock for Stephen. He had signed up to go on a biology field trip for extra credit. Chipping at sandstone, he exposed the remains of a six-inch fish preserved on both planes of cleavage. He gave one half away to a friend. I was framing the half he kept, for Christmas. The young man helping me had been as thrilled to help as Stephen was to find the fossil. He suggested an oak frame and blue matting, cut the backing and eight side pieces, knotted the fish line to secure the rock in place and glued the double frame together.

"A young man helped me before," I said.

"That was probably Brent. He's dead."

I could see Brent in my mind—fair-haired and blue-eyed. "Leave the box with me for a few hours," he had said, "while the glue dries." Brent had helped me simultaneously with a dozen others all finishing projects for the holidays.

"It didn't seem that hard before," I said. I tried to think about the shadow box.

"Well, it is and Brent's not here. I told you, he's dead."

The first comment I tried to endure, but torturing me twice was too cruel. I couldn't look at her. I spent the next two hours shaking with a mixture of anger and heartache. "Doesn't anybody care about them?" I missed Brent, then I missed Stephen; I grieved for young death.

"What kind of person can talk that way about tragedy?" I asked at dinner.

It was weeks before I returned to the shop to finish my

project. I considered patronizing another store but materials had been ordered. I hoped the woman would not be there—maybe she had been fired. After an hour, she came out from the cutting room to assist an older customer. She was skilled and made helpful suggestions. I nurtured my grudge. I was proud of being civil to the woman.

Months later I was at the frame-it shop again, working on family photos until the last minute before closing. Other employees brought in a birthday cake for the woman. They talked about her past. I learned she had spoken candidly about tragedy because she had been familiar with it her whole life.

That's when I missed Stephen the most! I was ashamed. Stephen would have defended the woman's worth with his glance. He would have dissuaded me from shallow judgment.

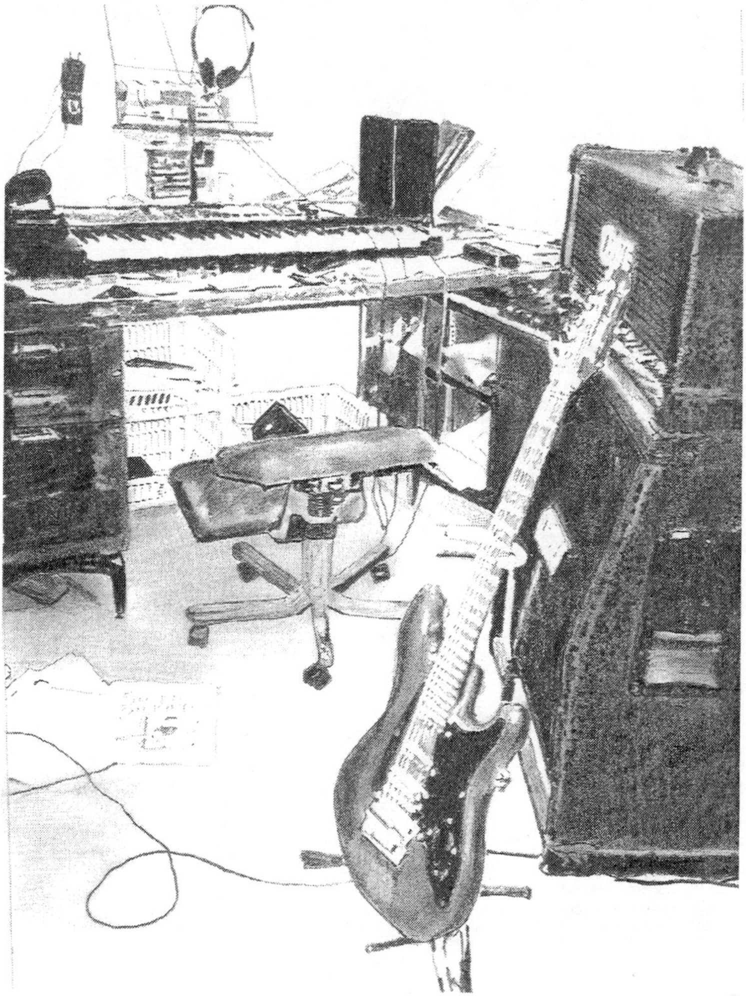

sixteen

Falling

Stephen spent $36 on groceries a week after Thanksgiving and gave them away to homeless people downtown. "Then," he wrote, "I bought an eclair, a cinnamon roll, a cookie, all of which I ate for lunch with another roll, milk, two oranges and lots of icing. Then I ate a good sized dinner with three cookies for dessert...I haven't played much guitar, I didn't exercise today and often I feel like I'm several different people. If I kept this up for another six months, I'd be dead."

He fasted two days for a friend with lupus and then got angry at himself for eating a big dinner.

"Mom, I can't make it through the winter here," he said. "I'm falling apart."

That day we made plans for him to go to Arizona and work for a stereo parts company. He drove down after Christmas in his small pickup truck with 87,000 miles on it that he had purchased for $800.

After working for six weeks he wrote a letter to us he never sent. "I've been doing things I don't like for so long that I've lost my senses. I don't know if I'm happy, sad, bored, tired, hungry or anything. I kind of feel like a fish who's just been gutted and now he's not even sure he's really a fish.

"Life was too hard with my old personality so I've pretty much taken all my beliefs that slow me down and thrown them away. The only things that I've kept that I'm aware of is my love for music, healthy food, and desire to be great.

"The reason I've had to change is because I couldn't keep going. I'd drive myself crazy. In order to sanely live twenty-four hours a day without picking up escape habits, I have to think differently. I can't expect too much out of myself, I can't think I can change the world in a day…if someone did, it would collapse the next."

He bought a new keyboard in March, quit his job in Arizona, and drove home. On a mild Saturday evening when we had guests coming to dinner, he walked in and swung me off my feet by the oven where french bread was baking. "I'm glad to be home, Mom." He carried in from his truck seventeen plastic grocery sacks full of grapefruit and an old pink suitcase of oranges. "Your niece sent the oranges and the grapefruit are from an orchard down her street. The owner said I could pick all I wanted."

Stephen and Mike played basketball with the outside lights on until 11:00 P.M. when they headed downstairs to talk business. Stephen wanted Mike to be his partner when he finished college, marketing his music or starting an import business. Mike had just completed winter quarter at the "U"; they planned to do things together everyday until Mike entered the Missionary Training Center—overnight stays at a cabin, hiking, lunch at a new Italian restaurant.

Stephen envied Mike, not because he was leaving for a mission—he realized that was impossible for him—but he feared making no measurable progress in the years Mike was gone. Most of his goals hinged on lucky breaks beyond his control. Since he wasn't sure what he would be successful doing, he kept exploring possibilities.

At night I stayed in the kitchen. Stephen wanted to talk. "People my age have gotten jobs teaching English in Taiwan. Do you think I could do it?"

"Sure, there are classes available teaching English as a second language," I said.

"Would I have to take a class?"

"No, but it would make you more confident." Stephen looked discouraged.

Traveling would open up new opportunities he wanted. Last December he had planned to save for a round trip ticket to Australia but he spent his winter earnings on a sound computer keyboard.

"The best thing Stephen did this winter was earn the keyboard," his employer said.

"Didn't he work hard for you?" I asked.

"He held on."

I remembered Stephen giving notice to an employer only once before quitting a job, and this wasn't the time. He had eight bosses that he worked for until he couldn't stand it another moment, then walked out or moved away.

A week after Stephen returned, the whole family including grandchildren went down to his bedroom after dinner for a sound computer demonstration. He cued up wild animal noises, rainy day effects, and symphonic voicings.

"Why don't most musicians make it big? Can't I market my own music? Why do I need more training?"

"Stephen's pressing me for answers he doesn't want to hear," I told Lloyd. "We can't talk reasonably anymore. I just frustrate him."

I shifted my writing to the bedroom desk. One night I

came into the kitchen and found Stephen holding a sewing needle in one hand and a grip of his chest skin in the other. "Stephen, don't be mean to yourself."

"I just like to see how well I can take pain." He walked away into the unlighted dining room. For Cathy's wedding he had a self-inflicted black eye that couldn't be camouflaged with make-up. Mike had explained to me. "Stephen just got angry at himself and kept hitting his face."

"Stephen, since you're not afraid of pain," I said, "would you help John pull his loose tooth?" Stephen had stood facing the cupboard getting a B-complex pill. He turned around quickly and spoke deliberately. "Only for myself, Mom. I could never hurt anyone else." I knew that wasn't true if he counted restoring justice, but this was no time to cross him.

At Mike's farewell meeting Stephen said, "I'm grateful we have our own lives and can make our own decisions. I'm glad to support Michael in his decision to go on a mission." After the meeting people crowded around Mike but more people were waiting to see Stephen—scout leaders, teachers, swimming students, employers, but also a line of older women who continued to adore him long after he quit working in their yards. Stephen was late getting home. I was already fixing refreshments in the kitchen for the relatives. He was jubilant, laughing. It was his job to mix the slush; he could hardly concentrate on the ingredients. "Did you see all those people who wanted to talk?" he said. "If ever there was a meeting for me, even more people would come."

Stephen and Mike tightened up their goals during their final week together, continuing to exercise daily and eat healthy food. Stephen planned to study on his own; Mike vowed to focus better on curriculum. Their long term objective was financial stability, then they could buy run-down houses to fix up, and a boat to share.

"It would be great to live next door," Stephen said. He and Mike were downstairs dreaming together. "Our kids could be best friends."

"And we will get our business going strong..."

"Then we'll probably have to hire employees..."

"How could we know they would be loyal?"

"Tests..." Stephen said, "we could test them bungie cord jumping or skydiving."

The day Stephen drove Mike to the missionary center they combined their errands—Stephen needed a new driver's license and Mike, film and day planner refills. We stood together at the end of the orientation admiring our sons' preferences that partings not be emotional, an attitude that dissolved in future weeks.

Stephen was turning the corner ahead of me toward the exit when a young instructor clasped his hand. "Getting ready for your mission?" he asked. "...It's never too late." Someone else cornered him outside. Suddenly the equal worth, the confidence Stephen had felt next to Mike was shattered unintentionally by those who were encouraging him to do something of which he was incapable. I was as sorry for Stephen that afternoon as I had been happy for him when the group gathered around days earlier at the farewell meeting. All the people who had talked to Stephen in recent days were well-motivated, but those who knew Stephen personally respected his decisions and encouraged him in what he thought was right. The others were making assumptions about his welfare. No wonder Stephen is so sensitive about judging, I thought. The people who don't know him well don't understand.

"Why can't people allow room for differences?" Stephen asked me when we arrived back home. He was still flushed. He stomped around the kitchen fixing himself a snack. "I'm going to have to avoid people who try to change what I am." Nothing, even in retrospect, could have kept Stephen from seeing Mike off that day. They were equally scared and eager to make a significant contribution with their lives. Stephen had hoped for equal support.

Stephen worked intermittently for a T-shirt company,

practicing music the other days. He compensated for time spent away from his younger brothers—slipping away with them to movies and the yogurt shop. He jogged regularly up the canyon and played basketball with Chris, the friend from New Mexico who rented half his room two years earlier. Chris still lived with us, in his own room. He was a premed student who played an intense ball game.

One night Stephen came home from work, showered, and entered the kitchen wearing a fresh shirt, cotton pants and top-siders. "Let's play ball," Chris said.

Stephen looked out the window at the dripping basketball hoop; rain pounded the cement. "Why not?" They played for an hour. During a break Chris put on a hat and Stephen took off his nice shoes with arch supports continuing barefoot, flatfooted. I sat on a stool in the kitchen and watched their craziness.

"We're going to the Mill this weekend," I told Stephen after his second shower. "The standard rules apply—no guests here while we're away."

Stephen laughed. "You still don't trust me."

"We have to be consistent," I said. "I tell Chris the same thing."

"To tell you the truth, Mom, now I care more about what you think than what I want."

Stephen helped Lloyd cue up the cello voicing on his sound computer so Lloyd could work on a composition. Late in the evening Stephen went into Martha's room. "I think I need to learn classical guitar, Martha," he said. "It's more listenable."

Martha never knew when he was serious. Before Mike left, Stephen had awakened her in the night complaining that his neck hurt. He turned on her light and twisted his head making awful popping sounds. She sat up worried until she saw Mike at the doorway and realized Stephen was biting raw spaghetti.

This time Stephen was in earnest. He wanted to start

learning a classical piece that moment. Martha played "Polonaise" from Bach's B-Minor Suite on her flute into the microphone. When she went to sleep, Stephen was picking it out on his guitar, listening to her recording. Frank had been married the day before. A guitarist played at the reception and Stephen had asked him lots of questions.

"Maybe we could play duets, Martha," he said the next morning. "Then we could play at receptions."

Friday morning, before we left for the Mill, I announced I was starting another diet—no desserts, no snacks, no eating after 7:00 P.M. "Mom, I will help you," Stephen said. "Don't even worry about fixing meals for the other kids. Just do what you need to." He was eating a slice of whole-wheat toast I burned, without butter.

"Can I have a girl over for breakfast Sunday morning before church?" he asked. I called Lloyd at the office. We always counseled about the children. Not only did I seek reaction from another vantage point, but I needed to be balanced by a different kind of mind. Lloyd was logical and objective. He loved the children as much as I did but he could see issues uncluttered by emotion. I loved our children in an intimate way, so tangled in their daily lives that my impulsive responses could inadvertently make me too tender or harsh. We agreed to Stephen's request—it was a fair exception to the rule.

It was a spring day full of errands and packing and check lists, strewn with ambivalence. One minute I wondered if we were foolish to take the weekend away—the next I was sure the retreat would lengthen our lives. Late Friday afternoon we backed out of the driveway; I thought about my recent conversations with Stephen. I felt assured that we had communicated completely with each other. Other times when I left, I think I had been at fault for not expressing my expectations. This time the rules were clear and best of all, the edgy issue of trust had ended in this morning's compromise. Stephen felt comfortable asking for an exception we could accommodate. And midpoint in the negotiating, Thursday night when I was already kneeling by my bed, he had come bounding in to show off the new top-siders he had bought used from a friend for $10. They were quality shoes he assured me—thick leather with excellent arches. He had been on one of his highs, dressed in his newly handmade designer shirt. He rarely popped into our bedroom like that; it was good to see him so happy and directed. I felt I could leave that weekend in peace. We were at a good stage in our relationship.

Stephen put in a full day Friday at the T-shirt company. After work, he spent a couple of hours with friends, ones who drank and had access to drugs. That evening Chris, who worked at the golf course across the street, found Stephen sitting on the curb worried about his dye-stained hands.

They walked in the house together about 10:00 P.M. Cathy and her husband had arrived just minutes earlier with a video, hoping that Stephen and Chris might want to watch it with them. We did not need to ask Cathy to look out for Stephen. She knew we had gone out of town that weekend; she always cared about him.

The TV in the kitchen was smashed. "What happened?" she asked. Stephen stared at it.

Cathy wanted to help him, to defend him, this brother who had always stood up for her—chasing a man through a parking lot who had stolen her wallet, igniting Barkley's dung on the porch of a boyfriend who had treated her rudely.

"Stephen stared at the TV in disbelief," Cathy said, "like he was trying to figure out what had happened." Stephen told them, "I think I broke the TV...Yes, I broke it. I broke it!"

"He paced around the kitchen," Cathy told us, "seeming to comprehend for the first time what he had done." She swept up the broken glass.

"I need Clorox to wash my hands," he said. "Is Emily sleeping over?"

He stirred frozen orange juice in a plastic pitcher. "Show

me something green," he said looking around the room.
"Show me something red."

Cathy said later, "His questions reminded me of a night in
high school when he had experimented with acid. I had taken
him for a drive while he wound down. He kept noticing
colors."

When the juice was dissolved and ready to pour, Stephen
knocked it over. Two quarts splashed on the table and down
to the floor. He jerked to meet Cathy's eyes, "Did I do that?"

"He could hardly believe what he had done," Cathy said.
"But the juice was all over."

"I did that!" he said. Then he persisted in asking all kinds
of questions.

"Who did Liz marry? What was her old boyfriend's
name? Is there a golf course nearby?"

"He seemed to be trying to comprehend what was real,"
Cathy said, "like I sometimes feel when I waken from a
dream."

Stephen walked out the back door. "We had never seen
him disoriented like that," Cathy said. "We followed him but
he was too fast. We circled around in our car looking, relieved
that he wasn't driving."

When Stephen came back an hour later, he was quiet.
Cathy's husband got out nacho chips and grated cheese,
stalling, trying to keep the mood light and help Stephen feel
comfortable. Stephen stood staring, two feet away. He talked
with Chris for a while on the back stairs and spent time in his
room. Cathy and her husband left in the early morning hours
when Stephen's door was closed and his light was off.

Cathy awakened Saturday morning worried about him.
She dressed quickly not taking time to shower; pondering
what to do. Then she just puttered around their home. She
talked to her husband, and to his grandmother about Stephen.
Her distinct feeling was to delay. Finally, she got in the car
and drove past our home on an errand. "I saw Stephen's truck
in the driveway and could have stopped in to see him then.

I've rethought it all. I kept feeling I should delay a little longer and give him room."

Stephen's truck was not in the driveway when she returned ten minutes later. She called Chris at the golf course. He had seen Stephen that morning, sitting at the kitchen table drinking a glass of water. He had looked tired and said nothing about working.

Then Cathy was nervous—she could not imagine where he had gone on a Saturday morning if not to work. She went down to Stephen's room; the door was locked. She ran upstairs, outside and around to the back stairwell that also accessed his room. His outside door was locked too; it was an old wooden door which had been forced open many times before. The handle was loose and Cathy shoved it open with her shoulder. His room was orderly, no different than the previous night. Then Cathy searched the rest of the house, the yard, and back around through everything a second time. After half an hour she called her husband. He knew she had a long list of errands.

"I can't believe you're still there," he said.

"I can't find Stephen."

She paced through the house again wondering if she should drive around the neighborhood looking for him. "I considered doing my other errands, hoping to somehow run into him…maybe at the grocery store like I had twice already that week…but I just couldn't leave the house."

She found the Mill number on a Post-it note in Lloyd's study and sat there by the phone, waiting. "I was so nervous…finally, I said out loud, 'Someone, please call.'" The phone rang minutes later. It was the social worker from the hospital; he explained that Stephen had been in an accident.

Stephen had jumped off a downtown parking plaza into an empty alley. A policeman was thirty feet away. While the ambulance came, Stephen spelled his name for the officer.

The internist talked with me on the phone, while I was still at the Mill. "It's serious," he said, "but I think we can save him." Cathy met Stephen in the emergency room. She held his hand and told him how much she loved him, how much our family loved him. "He had the same look in his eyes," Cathy said, "as he did the night before when he saw the smashed TV...like he couldn't believe what he had done."

I called a leader in our church and asked him to give Stephen a blessing. When we arrived at the hospital Cathy was tranquil. "The prayer calmed us," Cathy said, "Stephen stopped hyperventilating." While the operation continued we discussed plans for his recuperation. There was a clinic in Arizona where Stephen could go when he was released; they would evaluate his chemical deficiencies as well as provide therapy. We were optimistic when Lloyd left the waiting room for information on the progress of the surgery. He returned with the doctor in charge of the trauma unit. Stephen had died on the operating table.

For five minutes inhibition in me ceased to exist. I wailed in anguish holding to Lloyd. My life was severed by the shock of his death; all earlier events would be separated from my life ahead by this vacuum in time.

The doctor was still standing there when I reentered reality. He explained the details of the surgery. The anesthesiologist joined him. The internal surgery had been completed as planned but they had found a wad of aspirin in his stomach. The orthopedic team was ready to begin when "his heart just stopped," the doctor said. "It was strong one minute and then there was nothing. None of our efforts could stimulate another heartbeat."

The night before, Stephen had written notes. "I think too much. My brain won't stop. It won't look at things the same way as others. I'm falling. I've always had problems and I don't want to. I want to do everything but there isn't enough time in life. I believe in you Mike."

In the morning he wrote, "I love you guys. $ for the TV. Dad, you have all my equipment."

Cathy is still too tender to confront Stephen's death. She couldn't read what I wrote or discuss the details. She had the hardest role shortly before and after he died. People kept saying to her, "Don't feel guilty. It wasn't your fault." She listened. She hadn't felt guilty until so many people kept mentioning it. "I began wondering," she said, "if I was supposed to, if I had done something wrong." Over a year later she told me, "Even you, Mom…on the day of the funeral when I walked into the kitchen and you were discussing that awful newspaper article that had everything wrong about Stephen—that misquoted me—I asked why you hadn't shown it to me and you said, 'We didn't want you to feel guilty.'"

I can't remember saying that to Cathy. I did not know what she was feeling. I think it must be a natural but hazardous reaction to assume that the people closest to unnatural death have reason to feel guilty. Cathy has been an important part of my healing. She was more sensitive to Stephen during his life than I. Knowing she was close to him, watching over him during his last hours, assured me I could have done nothing more.

I knew I had to deal honestly with Stephen's death. I had to accept the reality that he could have taken drugs on Friday night, in spite of his clean record in recent months—that would account for his irrational behavior.

"He just got angry," Mike sobbed. "If I had been there, I could have saved him."

I spoke at his funeral. "Stephen's slip Friday night hurt him so deeply, he didn't think he could rise up. He despaired."

The medical examiner's report came back two weeks later. There was no trace of any drug in his system. I sat in the warm parked car alone with the window down, holding the truth on the papers in my hands. I read it over and over. Why hadn't I trusted him?

"I'm sorry, Stephen," I cried aloud.

"Experience is like the stern lights of a ship," Coleridge said, "which illumine only the track it has passed."

I didn't have the experience to understand Stephen's problems and I'll never have all the evidence to understand his death.

In the summer sun, I walked through the pastures near Bear Lake with a friend. She told me, "I sat at Stephen's funeral and thought my son was being described."

"Stephen wasn't a suicidal type," I said.

"Do you understand 'manic depressive'?" she asked.

Her question revived my memory of standing in the kitchen with Stephen the morning after the sewing needle incident.

"Stephen, you scare me sometimes," I had said. He was making a sandwich for his lunch.

"Mom, you know I'm schizo."

"No, I don't know that."

"There's another side of me you never want to see," he had said.

"But he was doing so well—" I told her, "working, jogging, practicing—he had all kinds of plans."

"That's the problem," she said. "Their periods of manic excitement alternate with melancholic depression and the lows directly follow the highs, feeling deeper and more hopeless each time."

Stephen's last journal entry read, "There are so many things I want to do in this life. I want to build speakers, roam Australia, tour the world, be an engineer, run a marathon, eat Jell-O, meet all types of people, fly an airplane, sail the ocean, write a book, make movies, make music, make love, do back flips, and much more."

seventeen

Looking In

When I read in Stephen's journal about me, I was chagrined. "I was feeling a little nippy," he wrote, "because at dinner (and really always) Mom was just continually talking. I don't like being around people who talk all the time. They disturb me. I like silence and you kinda get frustrated when you can't get away from it."

Fair criticism, Stephen. The irony is that I don't like non-stop conversation either, but I grew up thinking dinner should be a learning time. My parents treated dinner like a meeting. No one left until they were excused and that wasn't until after Father, who ate slowly and led discussions on world affairs and local news, had swallowed the last piece of the last cookie and wiped his mouth. At dinner I was taught to ask intelligent questions and logically examine issues. In spite of the frustration it caused me, I knew that I had learned most of the useful information I took into adulthood around the kitchen table.

Life ever since has been teaching me the importance of silence. Lloyd told me the third day of our honeymoon, which consisted of driving from Utah to Washington, D.C., that it was all right if there were times when neither one of us spoke. I was relieved.

A decade later I had wanted to be a quiet observer inside the Dome of the Rock. Our tour guide in Israel during the spring of 1976 was Mohammed, one of millions of Arabs with the same name. Outside Jericho we had driven in the tour bus past a vacant Palestinian refugee camp.

"Why is it empty?" a business executive asked. He was dressed like a tourist in a plaid sport shirt. Mohammed explained there was no food or work nearby. The people could not survive.

"Do you feel safe in Israel?

"Are you restricted by the Israelis?

"What will happen to the Palestinians here?"

The same man kept asking questions. Mohammed was polite. I was uneasy. The 1973 Arab attack on Israel during Yom Kippur had further heightened Arabs' and Jews' distrust of each other. We had felt the tension while crossing the border from Jordan into Israel. My mother in front of me had slumped onto a chair when she saw the five-foot pile of sand bags topped by Israeli soldiers lying with their rifles in firing position.

With the tourists in the bus, Mohammed had seemed to choose his answers carefully. But in Arab-dominated Hebron, he was carefree, joking with the street vendors selling toy drums and brass lamps. In Old Jerusalem, he stayed by the bus, avoiding the Jewish populace.

"What do you think of Yasir Arafat?" the executive asked Mohammed as we drove to the Temple Mount.

"I don't really know," Mohammed said more slowly this time, continuing to look out the front window. I wondered how a Palestinian could safely answer any of the questions this man was asking, even in a bus.

Mohammed watched while we went to the Wailing Wall of Herod's Temple but he caught up with us on the way into the mosque. Our shoeless group gathered on thick Persian carpets, looking at the octagonal dome of delicately inlaid wood. Then the executive approached his wife from behind and laughingly put his arms around her, rocking back on his heels.

"We allow none of that here!" Mohammed blurted out. "This place is sacred."

I half heard the rest of the presentation. I was embarrassed for the Harvard-trained executive. I felt lucky not to have naively done anything similar.

As I look back, I think the executive might have been more sensitive in the mosque if he had not been surrounded by an American tour group. They made him feel too comfortable. I feel the same way at home around the dinner table. But when I'm an isolated stranger, I keep quiet figuring out what is appropriate. Silence protects me and invites others to speak.

Three summers ago, Lloyd and I took Martha and John to the Pow Wow on a reservation in Idaho to see our Shoshone foster daughter, Lona, who had come to live with us a year before. She was short in our family and had an enigmatic countenance. We never knew what she was thinking until she spoke—even then we weren't sure. Lona had told us we could camp, otherwise we would have hesitated setting up our tent in the fairgrounds parking lot between huge teepees and log shelters. It was already dark. We worked in the beam of our headlights.

Electric bulbs dangled from booths where fast foods and silver jewelry were sold, encircling the main arena where the native dance competition was in progress. Dancers of all ages in beaded cloth and feathers moved to the drum beat, paper armbands displaying a competition number on one side and a Coors beer ad on the other. Groups of musicians from different tribes huddled in circles around the perimeter of the cement floor. As one group finished, the next began, chanting, beating the rhythm. We stood at a portal watching others go in and out before venturing into the sparsely occupied bleachers. No one was drinking. We learned that alcohol was banned on the reservation.

Lloyd and John saw Lona at the taco stand. "She hardly seemed to recognize us," Lloyd told me. She did not meet us at 11:00 P.M. as she agreed. She had eluded us the whole weekend.

On top of my sleeping bag, restless on clumps of sage brush, I listened to the beat of drums. I tried to imagine what the chanted words meant. The next morning a Navajo man who used the portable toilet shed after us explained there were two kinds of chants—sacred, which we would never hear, and tales, some traditional and some improvised. A wrinkled woman, wrapped in a colorful blanket, smiled at him from her lawn chair in front of their shelter.

"It's all in the rhythm and way you use your voice." He slapped his truck hood and chanted slowly about a man heading to Florida to find his aged mother.

We drove out the gate of the fairgrounds. A local Shoshone collected entrance fees from the few other white people entering. All Native Americans entered free. We found our foster child's house less than a mile away. A large solemn woman admitted us and got the father to come to the door.

"No, she never came home last night," he said. "She's like that sometimes."

We walked over the clean yellow linoleum to a carpeted room with two large recliners in front of a TV and one sofa. We sat lined up on the sofa and the father pulled a recliner around to face us.

"Well, you can't find her," he started again. "She has

problems, but not like her sister." The father told us that the daughter, who lived with us during the school year, had been in an accident with her boyfriend's car "driving under the influence." She had a date to appear before the tribal leaders after school started in August.

"Isn't she coming back to live with us?" John asked.

The father looked at John but did not answer. "The schools here are no good. I want her to go away to school. There is no work here. I got another job two months ago off the reservation. I work at a refinery thirty miles away. I go when they call—anytime, often in the middle of the night. Sometimes I work twelve hours. It's hard, dirty, but I need to do it."

He relaxed, pulling a leg up over his other knee and pushing back in his chair. John was restless; I hoped he would not ask more questions.

The father gazed around the room. "Alcohol is a big problem. I almost died twice on the street before I dragged myself into the Rehab Center. The girls' mother is still out there, somewhere. She's been gone five years."

I sat motionless, hoping we could be unobtrusive enough for him to continue.

"It's hard in the Center. The walls are all white. The stink comes out all over your body. For days you lie in the stink. You want to get out. They do not make you stay. The second time, I knew if I left I would die, so I stuck it out."

Now he was engrossed in his story. I wondered if he remembered we were there.

"People talk to you in the Center but you can't say anything for days. You hear them but you can't speak. When the poison is all out they talk to you more. They tell you it will be hard outside but you can make it." The father looked past us to the white wall with two high windows.

"I am dry for five years now but I am still afraid."

"Have you told your daughter these things?" Lloyd asked. "Maybe it would help her."

"No," he said. "She will have to learn herself."

The day after Stephen died I sat alone at the dining room table for hours with the drapes closed. The doorbell kept ringing. Emily, noticeably pregnant with her second child, had come over to help. She wrote down on a pad of yellow paper the names of visitors and what they brought.

"Is there something I can do?" I heard my neighbor say.

"You have," Emily told her. "My parents will be grateful you came."

"I don't know how to help," my friend said.

"They know you care."

Sometimes Emily came in and sat by me. "Are you okay, Mom? Do you want to go into your room and lie down?"

I was content to listen. I wanted to hear the visitor's thoughts. I wanted to hear Emily graciously answering their questions. It was all comforting, so long as I could be quiet, observing without being seen or touched or leveled by emotion.

The night before I had not slept. I had stayed alone on the sofa in the dark living room waiting for some resolution, some explanation of Stephen's death. My young sons wandered upstairs and laid their blankets on the floor beside me. John finally drifted off to sleep near morning but Andrew jolted upright every few minutes. About midnight, when we were all gathered around the kitchen table, he had asked the significant question. "Does this mean Stephen can't live in the Celestial Kingdom?"

I had spent the night in silence, listening. A sort of nothingness had settled around me. I guessed it was because Stephen was in a spirit prison. There was no comfort in that. I would accept justice.

"But don't punish him," I cried, "when he's already contrite. You must know his heart!"

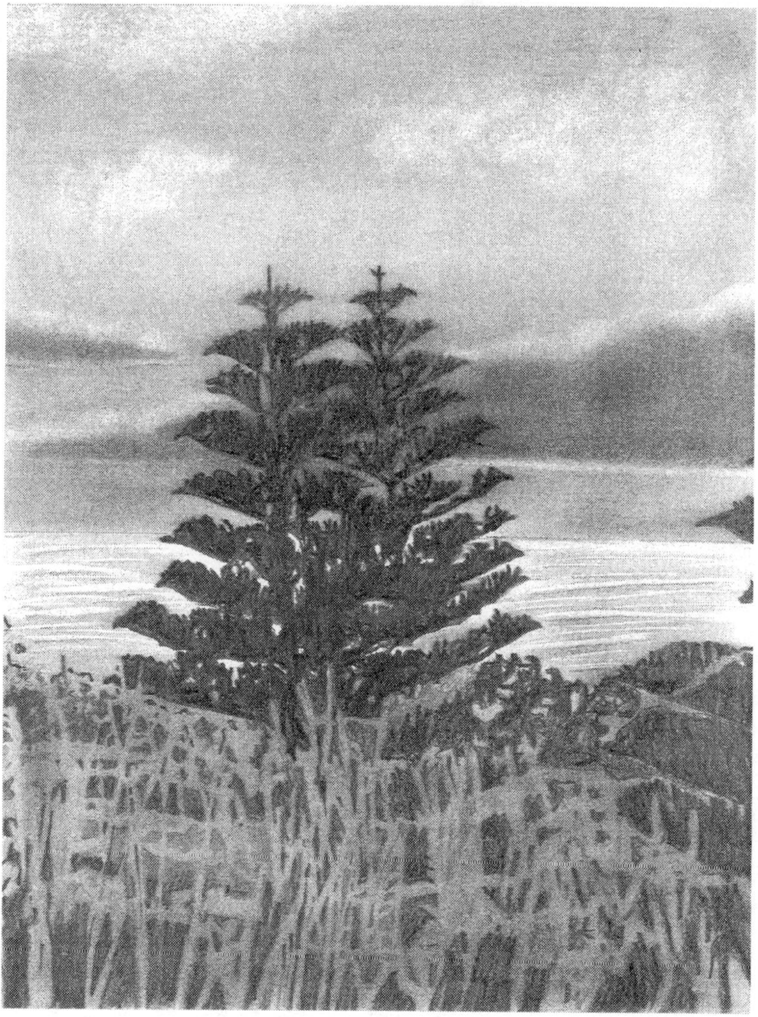

eighteen

A Roll of Film

With no relief Mother's Day dawned incompatibly clear and glorious. I couldn't stop crying and the sun wouldn't stop shining. Whipped by sorrow, still I couldn't deny the beauty around me. The birds continued to sing; they didn't irritate. The flowers, the fragrance of blossoms continued to exist resolute in their places but I couldn't respond to them.

The night of Rebecca's wedding, four years earlier, I had stayed on the sofa in misery too. My regrets had grown in the darkness. I had relived the day; intermittent rain had moved me to clean the downstairs (Plan B) two hours before the reception started. The caterer was in jeans the whole evening. She had no assistant, and forty pieces of chicken cordon bleu were cooking in the oven when guests filled the living room. Ten minutes later the chicken was sliced and jabbed with toothpicks but an hour later I remembered there were no napkins on the serving table. The groom's family turned into kitchen help washing plates in a sink clogged with carrot peelings. There was no ice to save the vegetables from drying under the emerging sun next to a bowl for dip that was empty most of the evening. I had turned on the light next to the sofa about 2:00 A.M. to restore normal size to my worries.

On the glass table in front of me were two huge baskets—one tilted inside the other abounding with Queen Anne's lace. The white blossoms were as big as my hand; they looked out in all directions from curves around oval handles. Only green shoots and ferns accompanied their delicate forms. The flowers, which celebrated Rebecca's marriage, had the potential to calm me. I had studied them. I looked from the base of each stem up to the node where it divided into spikelets and then sprayed into mists of blooms like fireworks.

For months afterwards I had sponsored flowers. I picked and arranged them to sit on the kitchen table, the mantle, the sideboard at the Mill, and then took photos to preserve them. I knew I was on a campaign for beauty.

This was the same sensation I had felt when I put my head under water in the Caribbean. On our trip to Mexico we had followed two native boys walking to the untrafficked side of Isla Mujeres. Carrying snorkels and spears, they went to the deep edge of the fringing reef to fish. We were short one pair of flippers so I sat down on the shallow edge while Lloyd and the children snorkeled nearby. They kept popping up with exclamations. I couldn't wait any longer. I put on a mask and leaned into the water. The rock beneath me transformed into living coral. Translucent ribbons swayed next to red and green feathery clumps. Bright sea stars clung to the ocean floor. Darting back and forth were blue fish with yellow foreheads, and further away, striped ones. We were in a paradise. We all knew it was worth the 8,300-mile drive, if only once.

The next summer we had explored the Canadian Rockies. We drove on Going-to-the-Sun road as far as Logan Pass and started hiking at 6,700 feet. Park wardens encouraged hikers to carry bells as protection from grizzlies. We carried a bull horn instead that the children blew before they rounded curves in the trail which wound past meadows of wild flowers. Even at this elevation whole forests were foreground to mountain ranges. We took turns snapping pictures of each other in "climb every mountain" poses with outstretched arms and open mouths. Waterton-Glacier Park was as spectacular as Switzerland; glaciers had formed peaks like the Alps.

Lloyd carried sandwiches, fruit, trail mix and hard candy. We ate it all. The children were tired.

"But there are huge mountain goats ahead, bighorn sheep," I said. "Don't you want to see them?"

"It's beautiful here," Rebecca answered. She was the oldest child with us. "We're happy where we are. You go on."

Lloyd followed me and Stephen ran to catch up, passing us both on the next hill. We were above the timberline. Yellow and orange lichens splotched cliffs; purple phlox grew in niches. We hadn't gone another half mile when we sighted the goats. Their white fur captivated us.

"I can go closer," Stephen said.

He hiked straight up methodically, carefully. The goats stared at him. From our view it appeared Stephen could pet them when he finally stopped to take a picture. Passing hikers encouraged us to go another quarter mile.

"The bighorn sheep are around the bend." Stephen acted refreshed. Eight sheep grazed, horns curled around their heads. One wandered onto the trail. We were quiet not to frighten them—I felt reverent.

Walking back down the trail I was caught between exuberance to have shared the experience with Lloyd and Stephen and disappointment that the other children missed it.

Even when we described the big animals no one else seemed to regret their decision to not go further. In our absence they had watched hoary marmots at play, and red squirrels.

In total, there was no question but what each child with us that summer was infused with nature. If they didn't soak it in hiking, or canoeing on Lake Louise, they did descending the Columbia Ice Fields. Stephen asked the guide if we could walk back from the bus mobile to the visitors center. The tour had taken us to the crest of the glacier; the ice seemed firm and dense. With permission we walked like giants over blue mountain ranges. Caverns went down hundreds of feet to crystalline waterways. We laughed, jumped and slipped down the 43-degree decline; I questioned the prudence of the young guide.

That was the second summer Emily had missed a "once only" vacation. She had been too afraid to accompany us on the Mexican trip to the Yucatan; we left her in Arizona with cousins. While we were in Canada, she was living in California with her birth family. The next spring I asked, "What about the Baja?"

A businessman had told Lloyd about Escondido Bay, two thirds down the peninsula. His description of sea life matched the Caribbean; it was the same latitude. Previously we had traveled as far as Ensenada and imagined the Baja would get more beautiful the further south we went. We could pick Emily up outside Palmdale and go straight south. She would feel safe with us in the motorhome going somewhere proximate.

The Gringo's Guide said "Bahia Los Angeles is a long day's drive from San Diego." The Bahia looked about half way down on the map that unfolded from above my head, lay across my lap, and dangled on to the floor with one section still covered. I ignored the time it would take us to get from Palmdale to San Diego and from the Bahia Los Angeles down to Escondido Bay.

"Let's just round it off as a day's drive," I told Lloyd and the children.

We drove through the night from Salt Lake to California and picked Emily up by 9:00 the next morning. The old motorhome was loaded with food—no delays grocery shopping. We crossed into Mexico just after noon. Ensenada was 45 miles further.

"We're doing great," I said.

Then the Transpeninsular Highway narrowed. It had no shoulders and few places to pull off. Mountains continued outside Ensenada. Sierra San Pedro Mórtir was over 10,000 feet high and we skirted it, straining to maintain an ascent at 30 mph. Both air conditioners were on high and we were perspiring.

I glanced at a road sign: Santa Rosalia 722, La Paz 1325. Our goal to Escondido Bay was between them. I knew kilometers looked oppressive. I didn't bother to figure out the distance in miles.

"Thank goodness we don't have to go as far as La Paz," I told Lloyd.

I moved up to the front of the motorhome where I could see the full panoramic view. "At first glance the desert is monotonous," I read to myself from the guide map, "but on closer inspection the true detail of life becomes obvious. Nature has engineered a diverse portfolio...cacti." I learned that a cactus in the Baja might just look like one in Arizona. "Most of it is endemic...found nowhere else because of the ruggedness of the environment." Hours later one of the children asked me, "When will we start seeing flowers and palm trees?"

Bahia Los Angeles was not on our way but we would be driving inland for two more hours and it seemed worth the side trip to glimpse an oasis and let the children swim. At 6:00 P.M. we descended to the Sea of Cortez. Not even cacti were there; the children ran over rocks and dirt into hot water.

"What kind of beach is this?" Emily asked.

We were sloshing around in the bay when someone

noticed sting rays. The boys chased them until a man came toward us in tennis shoes. He was the only person anywhere around. "They don't just sting," he said. "See those whipping tails? They cut."

We continued to drive after dark. We passed five towns listed on the map which weren't big enough to see. Once we paralleled the eastern coastline I described to the children the gray whales. Pointing into the darkness I explained, "They migrate here 5,000 miles from the Arctic Sea."

It was 2:00 A.M. when we drove into the lighted parking lot at Escondido Bay which was an oasis like we had heard. Flowers had been planted between curbs. Three palm trees grew by a walkway leading to the swimming pool. Now we knew that the people who patronized this place either flew or sailed there.

Lloyd returned from a walk to the pier before breakfast. "The only access to the bay is by boat," he said. "There are no boats for rent."

Nine of us walked out onto a floating dock hoping someone would notice. A young man drove his father's yacht out around the pier. Lloyd went over to try to negotiate with him. He looked past Lloyd to our four teenage daughters.

The young man took us deep sea fishing. We caught cabrilla which he filleted and fried for lunch. Anchored in a cove we snorkeled like we remembered doing in the Caribbean. We knew the underwater landscape was true beauty because it got better the closer we examined it and this time we had a guide. The clown fish had yellow foreheads and the angelfish had stripes. Mike pulled a "bivalve" off the coral wall for inspection. Our guide said it was a scallop.

"Can we cook it?" Mike asked.

"You'll like it raw," he said, cutting the meat into tiny pieces.

Something amazing was happening, besides the fact that Stephen was sunburned only on the back of his calves and neck. We were dwarfed in nature's magnificence; at the same time we were elevated because we could appreciate it.

The next day we hiked cross country to an inlet. Stephen strode off in thongs. We found him halfway to the water stuck on one of those endemic cactus—a large needle ran all the way through his big toe. Lloyd extricated him with fingernail clippers; they stayed together and took turns pulling the needle out. The rest of us wore shoes. We couldn't help so we went on down to clear the seaweed that covered half the water. Rebecca and Mike dove in; they pulled the growth to one side, giving us a private lagoon. Now we could see the advantages of a sparsely populated, desolate peninsula. Fragile species survived. The sea floor was a plethora of anemones, sponges and polyps. Stephen found an asteroid with orange discs that blended into purple at the thick center. Hermit crabs and sand dollars were plentiful. Later that morning Rebecca felt sick—a rash blistered her body. Then Mike noticed he was itchy. The seaweed was saturated with tiny jellyfish.

Listening to the children talk that evening and as they later recalled our trip, I wondered if the beauty in the sea had been enhanced by being hard to find. The motorhome stunk by the time we arrived home. I forgave Stephen for keeping the star fish and hiding it in a bread sack under the towels.

My campaign for beauty ended five years later on a trip with our youngest four children and Lona. Lloyd couldn't leave his law practice that spring so Mike and I drove the others to California for Easter break. We went to the beach two days, then to Beverly Hills, Universal Studios, and, on Friday we would go on to Tiajuana. I saved a half day for the Getty Museum, my preference over everything else. We parked on the Pacific Coast Highway in Malibu and walked between the pool and sculptured gardens past bronze statues to the replica of Villa dei Papiri, a Roman country house. The boys hesitated briefly when they saw snails by the hedge. We entered from the east into a round vestibule with glass enclosed Greek antiquities.

"Look how athletic they were," I said. I pointed to reddish figures racing around the curve of a black vase.

"See the guy with wings," Martha said. "I think I studied about him."

Lona was standing by a marble statue of a girl with her nose broken off. "This is weird."

Only Martha followed me into the atrium of Roman art. "We must go slower," Lona laughed in back of me.

The museum brochure showed paintings on the second floor so I walked slowly past the rest of the sculptures up the stairs and through the medieval exhibits. I paused when the religious art became lifelike and halted for the renaissance pieces, starting again until I found the impressionist works.

"The others must see this," I said. Martha volunteered to find them but I wasn't sure she had enough enthusiasm. We went back together. The boys were in the garden; they had found a frog. Lona was sitting by the pool.

"Let's go in! We've got incredible things to see."

"Not me," Lona said.

Now the others became immobile. I was angry. I had accommodated them and now they should support me. Besides, I was right. I told them, "This is some of the most beautiful art in the world."

"It's ugly," Lona said.

I took her firmly by the arm and headed for the museum entrance. The others followed closely. Part way up the stairs I said, "One half hour—that's all I ask. You don't understand what you're rejecting."

I pointed out the symbols of plants and windows in 15th century art. Lona was not impressed. We stood in a half circle in front of a Rembrandt while I described his concept of light. I stopped by a painting of Millet. "The impressionists chose to paint common people," I said. The half hour was nearly up when I saw *The Starry Night* by Van Gogh. I had never seen the original before; I hadn't expected to find it there. I could feel the darkness and the stars trailing paths of light.

"I'll be in the car," Lona said.

I was transported by the painting before me into a world of fantasy. "In my opinion…" I thought. Lona had made her point. Beauty is a matter of opinion for things other than nature.

Lona wasn't in the car when we returned. She was waiting on the sand watching the waves.

I didn't feel the need to push art or nature on my children after that. They would discover it better their own way. Stephen had brought two rolls of film home after his first job in Hawaii. He showed them to me after they were developed. One was of his dorm and outings to the beach. The other was of an identical scene—twelve pictures looking through trees and flowers to the water. The photos got slightly darker and richer as the sun set.

"Why did you take so many shots of the same thing, Stephen?"

He smiled. "It was so beautiful."

Lloyd felt the same compulsion when he saw the flowers on Stephen's casket. "We must take pictures," he said.

"No, this whole thing is too awful." I felt foolish immediately. The young man's mother who housed Stephen after he lived in the stone fort had created a masterpiece. The fragrance of torch ginger and yellow roses was diffused in mauve protea nestled between purple liatris and gold lilies. Ti leaves spread beneath and slightly protruding were blue and orange bird of paradise.

I realized I could experience joy from this casket spray which uplifted even as it blended with my helplessness. I felt a duality pulling at me as I faced this splendor. When Lloyd had said the flowers for Stephen were beautiful, he was speaking with a sort of universal voice, one that grief or pain should not silence. My pangs in those moments were a legitimate effect of beauty. Henry Van Dyke perceived "the secret pathos of Nature's loveliness. It is a touch of melancholy inherited from our mother Eve. It is an unconscious memory of the lost Paradise. It is the sense that even if we should find another Eden, we would not be fit to enjoy it perfectly or stay in it forever."

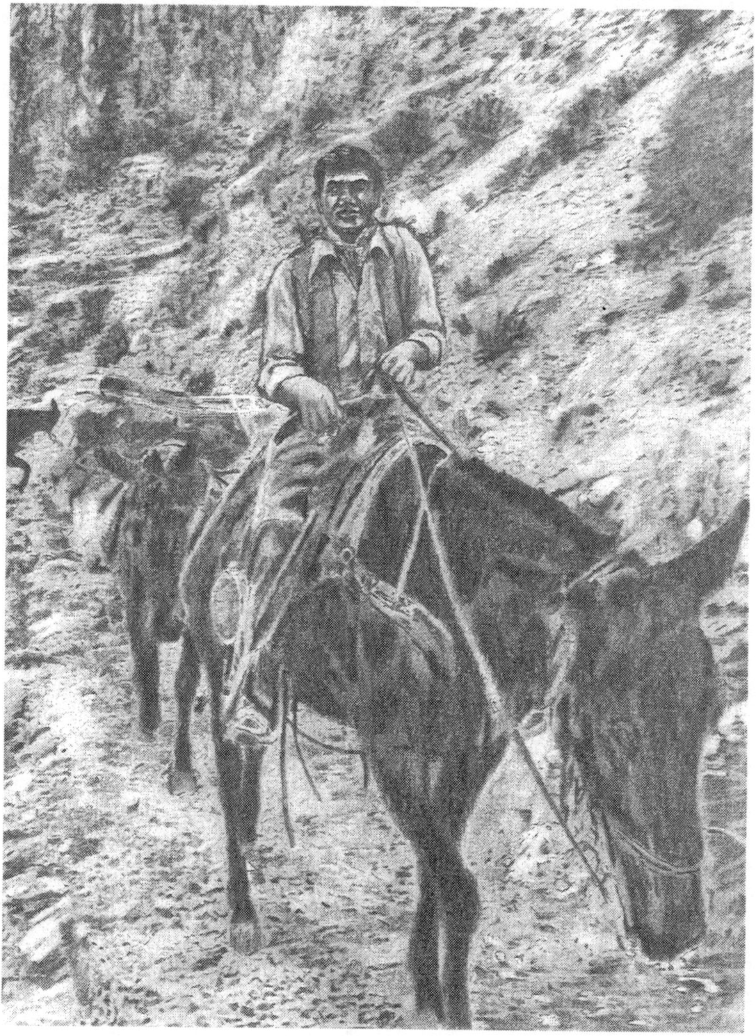

nineteen

Hitting the Wall

At the viewing I stood next to Lloyd, explaining to our friends who didn't know Stephen, "He wasn't a druggie, he wasn't mean and rebellious." But I would have loved him if he had been. I wished to say, "Don't be sorry for what we've been through. I wouldn't have missed a moment of Stephen's life with us." But there wasn't time to expand and I was too sad.

To others I said, "I admired my son." How could they believe me when I spoke about a young man who had caused his own death?

Then one of Stephen's reckless friends came through the line, one whom I suspected of influencing him adversely the night before he died. He waited in a suit and tie wiping tears from his face. I could hardly look up; Lloyd shook his hand.

A business acquaintance of Lloyd's stood behind him and told us later, "That friend of your son's said to me, 'Why did it happen to Stephen? He was the one who loved life the most!'"

The friend I misjudged. Struggling with his own problems, he understood! The ultimate grief was beating it into my heart. I must look beyond stages of development, stereotypes, divergency, to the things people have in common. I shared with that young man a friendship with the real Stephen, which was not the rarely-seen duality of his nature that killed him.

Typically, Stephen was, according to William James, a "sky-blue" optimist. On our last family vacation with Stephen, we rented a boat at Lake Powell, camping on the sand several miles north of Bullfrog Marina. While Lloyd and I were napping in the afternoon, all four sons went shell hunting.

"We found an inlet," John said, "with quicksand."

Stephen had gone in first, sinking, yelling and laughing. The others joined him and took turns jumping off a ledge high above their heads into the wet sand, seeing how deep they could go. After one of Mike's jumps, he waited sitting on his legs in the sand, shouting to Stephen who had appeared above him ready to jump again.

"Look how deep I am."

Stephen grubbed down into the sand to his waist before Mike stood up.

"Stephen kept laughing the whole time, but he couldn't get out by himself," John told me. "They made me stand on the other side while Mike and Andrew pulled him."

It was while sloshing back through the tepid water at dinner time, tripping on supposed rocks, that Stephen and Mike remembered they were shell hunting. The boys came toward us carrying over a hundred fresh water clams in their T-shirts. "We're bringing food!" Stephen called. He pulled the meat from each mollusk which finally made a tiny mound in the pan next to our dinner which had been ready for half an hour.

"Are we really going to eat these things?" I asked Stephen as I lit the stove again. "Of course, Mom, they're a delicacy!"

That same summer I had watched Stephen collapse on the porch after jogging. He fell onto the chaise lounge with one arm up over his face; he couldn't get enough oxygen. A rash blotched his body. I brought out wet towels, not saying much. I thought I knew what he was feeling and expected it would change him.

Several years earlier on a hot October day, eager that I could do something sporty with my children, I went to the school parking lot for the Clayton Junior High Marathon.

Many sports shame me. Lloyd pleaded with me to quit skiing until the children were raised. "Your daring exceeds your skill," he said. In tennis, I don't win matches with anyone over age twelve.

I had been regularly running a 2.8-mile route in the morning coolness for a couple of years. "This race is for adults too," Stephen kept reminding me. Both he and Mike wanted to run the three miles but were hesitant without family support.

I worried about whether I should eat a snack in addition to the high carbohydrate hashbrowns we had for breakfast, eventually drinking orange juice for lunch. At 2 o'clock the parents who were runners began arriving. I watched them stretch out their sinewy legs, relaxed and joking in nylon shorts.

Three hundred runners swarmed around the starting line. Rebecca had come to run with Stephen at a faster pace.

"Don't worry Mom, it thins out quickly," Mike said. The gun went off and after a few paces there was a place for me. The course started downhill. I consciously paced myself as the mass of children sprinted out of sight. Mike stayed with me. "We've got to run smart," I said. "Those guys ahead will be walking by the time they reach the hill," he added.

I was breathing through my mouth already. "We're doing great, Mom." We were just out a mile. The climb would last another. My lungs ached; I had to slow my pace. I urged Mike to go ahead. He hesitated, watching me sympathetically before moving on.

I tried to distract my mind and run automatically. More and more people passed me. Some dragged to a walk, like Mike had predicted, but then moved out again faster. The race felt like a character test; the thought of walking part way implied I was going backwards in my life.

I saw Rebecca's red T-shirt two blocks ahead. She was steady; her lead was not increasing. My throat was raw, rasping. I wondered if I would collapse on someone's front lawn, humiliating my children.

We hit the level stretch. I could hear the giddy cheering for finishers. The pain had gone. I was out of my body. It was running steadily without me. I could see my blurred children as I crossed the finish line.

My legs kept going over to the parked cars. I slid onto a fender, losing control of my body functions. Five minutes later I was able to focus when other mothers jogged onto the playing field, smiling and graceful.

An experienced runner told me later, "Now you know how it feels to hit the wall. Just keep running."

I stopped forever. My decision to finish running the race became, in William James's words, "an impossible fever and torment in me." I was burned out. I retreated, walking for exercise from then on.

Stephen kept running, passing walls. He believed in Martin Seligman's modern psychology for avoiding depression—"Let optimism benignly distort reality to give dreams and hopes and great plans room to flourish." I respected and feared the extremes Stephen pursued.

Sometime while raising my children, experience moderated my optimism; life was too hard for the "sky-blue" variety Stephen had. With him gone, I assumed an extreme of my own.

"Forget it," my trusted friend said. "You should just hear yourselves, it's pathetic. Everything we talk about comes back around to Stephen. You've had two months now and you've got to put it out of your mind." He had hosted us royally the night before—southern cooking served on the best china. He served breakfast on china too, rather than going to work, including our favorite grits. Lloyd looked at him but I could not; I focused out the window on the pines in the backyard. "But there is much," Lloyd said, "that I don't want to forget."

That night in Georgia I drove north through sparkling insects. The others slept. We had been on vacation for a week, relieved from daily reminders of Stephen. I had stored up too much; our ventilating appeared excessive. "Sure, just try to forget one of your children," I said outloud, banging the steering wheel. I finished a cup of ice, a sack of popcorn. And I was still preoccupied. He was right. I think about all my children in a day, but not all day.

We took our diminished family—Martha, Andrew, and John—to the bottom of the Grand Canyon. After hiking down thirteen miles with full packs, Lloyd and I took turns sleeping on a camping pad (the other one blew off the top of the car in Las Vegas). Lloyd wrapped my most damaged knee in an Ace bandage so I could limp to Mooney Falls. The next night I slept outside until one bat, then another, flew into my hair.

We stood in the sun by Havasu Falls to cool off before our return hike, watching our children and scores of agile youth jump from the rope swing and dive from mossy ledges into clear water. My pack went up on the mule train that morning—Lloyd called it a medical necessity. My swimming suit inadvertently went too.

I rolled my dirty pants up, determined to go as far into the water as possible. Lloyd, in his orange trunks, was ready for a swim. His thick, three-day beard gave him the charm of a rugged mountain man.

"You don't have to stand by me," I said to him. "I know I'm ugly."

"Why do you say things like that?" he asked.

I waded in the cool pools while Lloyd swam. Reality is valid, I thought. I look bad after three days on the trail. It's been a hard year psychologically.

But I knew I was wrong to cut myself down. There was a dichotomy in my nature too. The day before, when I ate dessert after a big dinner, I said, "I'm fat." When I forgot to prepare the PTA snack a week ago I said, "I'm stupid."

"What is crucial is what you think when you fail," Martin Seligman said for us living in the 90s. My ugliness was not permanent. Optimistically believing that setbacks are temporary revives hope. Years ago I let go of my dreams for Stephen, in order to accommodate his.

Yet, Seligman acknowledges that some pessimism is closer to reality. Almost a century ago William James did too. "The evil facts which the healthy minded [optimists] refuse positively to account for are a genuine portion of reality; and they may after all be the best key to life's significance and possibly the only openers of our eyes to the deepest levels of truth." Acknowledgment of my own failures preserved me but dwelling on them could destroy.

I walked painlessly up the Grand Canyon in the cool evening air not slowing anyone down until the switchbacks near the rim, when a mule knocked me off the trail.

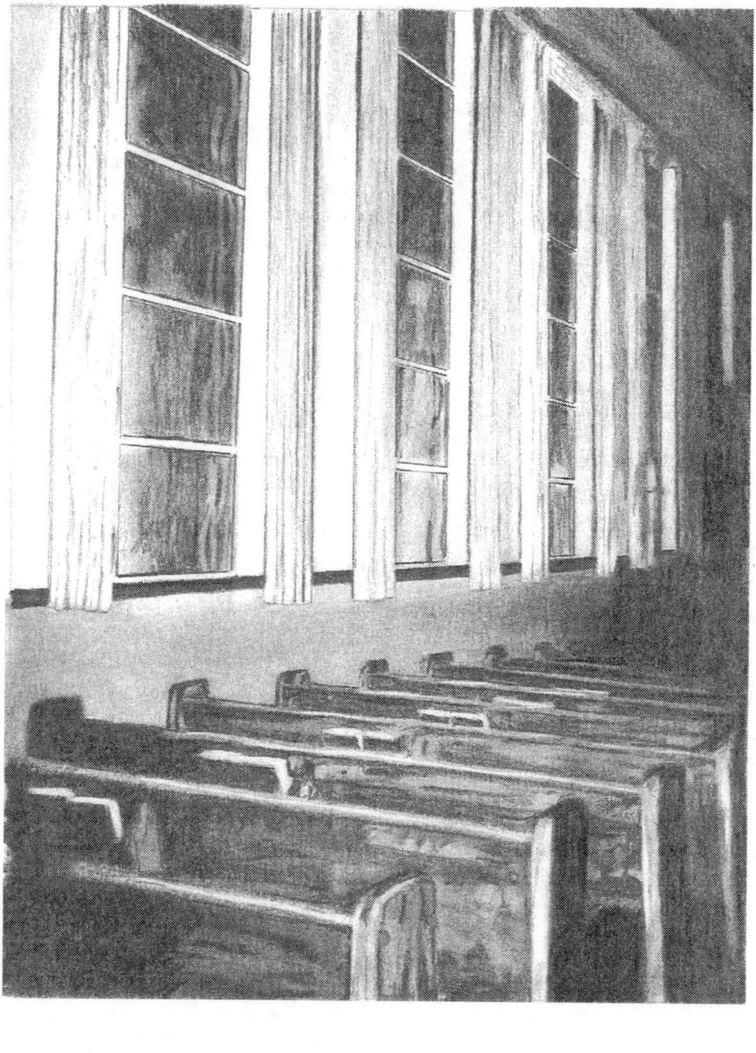

twenty

Sirens

The matter of violence, the quick destruction of a human life, demands my attention. "But not mine," said a student. We sat across the table from each other in a writing workshop. Stephen had been dead eight months. My classmate was irritated with everything I wrote.

"Why do you always choose topics that no one cares about?" he asked. "Death is not interesting to me." He is young I thought, inexperienced, and just as well for now.

When Stephen was my oldest preschooler, sirens converged outside our front door. From three emergency vehicles men rushed into the house across the street with their bags. Others followed with a stretcher. I pulled the blinds all the way up and watched. Oxygen had been delivered regularly to the man in that house whom I'd never seen. His wife was friendly, waving when she gardened in her front yard. The stretcher emerged through the front door with IV tubes already connected; there was blood on the sheets. It was noon. The music to Sesame Street had started on the TV. I was six months pregnant with Martha and knew I shouldn't leave the boys alone. The man was being lifted into the back of the ambulance. I pulled a box of crackers out of the cupboard for Stephen and Mike and slipped out the door.

The ambulance was gone. A policeman was talking with my neighbor and her adult daughter in the front doorway. I wondered what I was doing there.

"Can I help?" I asked.

"It's too horrible," the older woman said. "I was eating lunch in the kitchen and I heard a shot…"

"My father shot himself," the daughter finished. "We are on our way to the hospital."

"Is there something I can do?" I asked.

"I don't think so, dear," she said. "It all happened so fast."

"Will anyone clean up?" The policeman turned to me. "We won't be back."

"I'll take care of it while you're gone," I told my neighbor.

"You can't do it alone," she said.

"I'll get friends to help."

The policeman walked down the steps with me.

They left the front door open, closing only the storm door. I walked back across the street. What had I offered? Panic had gripped my mind as I watched the ambulance from my window; my body automatically rallied.

After an hour, when the job was reduced to buckets of pink tinged water carried from the living room back into the kitchen, my heart stopped pounding in my ears. I could relax. Two women, a marriage counselor and a mother of eleven, had come to help. They took turns telling stories to balance the melancholy in the house. Most of the stain had come out of the carpet. We covered the area with a fresh towel.

Stephen and Mike were down for naps when my neighbor returned. We talked on the phone. Her husband had died. I expected I would have nightmares but I didn't. The clean-up was a job that needed to be done, better by people removed from the heartache.

I did have nightmares the month before when our pipes froze and broke while we were away. Water above our ankles in the basement covered three rooms of new green carpet and two with parquet floors. The children splashed and laughed as they helped fill buckets, barefoot in winter. Stephen and Mike floated their plastic boats next to abandoned school papers until we passed the scooping stage, finishing with the wet vacuum.

We lifted the carpet before we turned on fans. The wood floor lifted itself, popping tiles as it dried.

The catastrophes had an unreal aspect that softened the crisis moments, like I was dreaming and would awaken later to normalcy.

When Stephen was eight, a teenage girl down the street telephoned me late on a snowy night. I trudged the short distance through drifts from my car to her house, stamping my feet before entering the warmth. In the back bedroom I helped the girl rouse her groggy mother, oblivious to mortal danger, and put on her fur coat and hat. Lined up together we stepped slowly out into the blizzard.

It was senseless to call an ambulance; we knew from experience what to do. The nurse at the hospital treated the mother, this friend of mine, like a naughty child, "You shouldn't do this—you know what we have to do now."

I sat with the black-haired daughter in the hall. "I can't stand to see her hurting," she said.

How could a fifteen-year-old girl comprehend what made her mother overdose? For years I had watched my friend's cycles as she rotated from pleasant and creative—writing, painting, crocheting—to being belligerent and abusive. Medication couldn't level her out. She was part of the World War II tragedy, terrorized by bombing as a young girl in Greece.

In Tennessee a phone call told me she finally took her life. I sobbed like Mike. "If I had been there…"

My sensitivity to casualties was measurable but not sufficient to help Stephen during the winter of his sophomore year in high school. He had gone sledding with friends behind the orthopedic hospital near midnight. On the first run he saw a car in the field below with lights on, the motor still running. The front doors were open and several feet away he found a girl, dead.

"Something was foul," Stephen said. "There were foot prints going off into the trees." The police investigated for hours. Stephen had come home in the early morning and awakened Cathy who was too tired to listen. Not wanting to disturb us, he went to a friend's house.

"I needed to talk with people who understood," he told me the next morning. The mystery of the girl's death magnified the shock. Had the girl been murdered? Should he and his friends be chasing someone? The police determined the girl had missed the turn on the road and rolled off the embankment, being thrown from her car and killed on impact.

"That's not right. You should have seen her, Mom. She was dead!" Stephen's voice cracked. He was angry that we didn't realize what he had been going through sooner. He thought that meant we didn't care, even that he drank alcohol in the night. Nothing he could do looked bad next to the girl's death. He would return to the scene again and again until fresh snow covered all evidence.

"Bad things happen to good people," I said at dinner, mostly to myself. I knew tragedy could be impartial.

A year after we moved back to Utah our friend Chester was made a Mormon bishop in Tennessee, only weeks before he was killed.

He had closed the town store on Friday night in Altamont, way up in the hills, and gone home alone. His wife Marjorie had driven off the mountain to help her daughter with a new baby. A son, back from college, came in later and was watching TV with his father when drunk men entered. The intruders bound them both, robbed Chester and finally shot him in the head.

Our family had spent a Pioneer Day with Chester. Opening the car in Altamont that July day, the muggy heat and hissing made me wish I had packed insect repellent. A rugged man with bright eyes in a face of bristles welcomed us. I could tell he was one of the eleven men Chester had activated in the church during recent months. He handed me a tin cup of clear liquid from a humming contraption roped off behind him. Confused, I brought it toward me. "Don't drink," he laughed. "It's for the tractor."

I read the hand-printed poster tacked to a board. "Moonshine, made for years in these mountains on outfits something like this…"

These leathery men could be trusted now; they were finding alternative uses for outlawed skills. As I watched them sweating patiently I could forget the violent past of the area. "Revenuers were killed razing stills up here," a man beside me said.

Gasohol was fueling a clean tractor running in the field. Down the hill in a shed targets were posted; I could hear muskets blast. Children stayed by the caged turkeys while Relief Society sisters in bonnets and polyester pants chatted next to displays of dried vegetables. Three caldrons simmered over coals. Chester was carefully stirring potatoes in oil with a fresh piece of lumber.

"Glad you came," Chester said, holding out a hand to shake. "Great day for a celebration."

A new chapel was to be constructed in Altamont. The old rock building didn't have indoor plumbing and was too cramped for the swelling congregation. Members of the church had sold anything lucrative to secure cash to contribute; some had even parted with their beds.

Like his parents, Chester had lived in Altamont all his life. He inherited the general store and passed around the town news. "I know if people keep their word up here," he said.

The children had been impatient for the turkey hunt; extras from the town arrived as the circle formed. When the gun sounded, they charged fiercely at the gray feathers. "It was all over before I touched one," Stephen said.

Chester took us in his truck to the lake while other vehicles followed, kicking up huge clouds of dust. The drive wound past shacks barely visible behind rusted bed springs and car parts, next to tidy homes. Eyes peered from porches and windows. I felt uneasy.

"Do you know all these people, Chester?" I asked.

"Not really, some people like to stay to themselves."

The lake was warm, large, and shallow on one side. A rickety platform fifteen feet high leaned toward the water. Men stripped to the waist revealed stark tan lines. They helped small bodies jump; everyone got wet.

Sitting on logs, we were teased by the aroma of stew. The men ladled huge portions into our styrofoam bowls. Marjorie glanced over. She had been busy all day but now she picked at her dinner like the rest of us. Countless bones revealed the pre-dawn bag of possum and squirrel.

"Thanks for your efforts," I said. "We've had a memorable day."

"It's the people around us," she said. "They've done it all."

Dancing and fiddling continued as Chester followed us to our car in the dark. "We're being blessed up here in Altamont," he said. "Aren't we?"

Ever since Chester's death I've wanted to sit on the logs in Altamont and eat greasy potatoes. I want to talk to Marjorie. I want to say, "Goodness can't be killed, it never dies."

The contrast between violent death and constructive life

shocks my soul and continues to pain me, but it shouldn't unbalance me. I shouldn't be defensive when Andrew's teacher calls him Stephen. We don't have to bury the substance of Stephen's life because his death is stigmatized by violence.

I wavered because suicide is darkness, rejection, a disease we fear might be contagious. The local high school started discussion groups amongst the students the Monday after Stephen's death, to avert imitative behavior. "Mom, a lot of young people think about it," Martha said.

And young people came to the funeral where the comfort of being "called home" could not assure. We sat together wondering if the gospel truth was big enough to make sense out of this calamity when the lightning flashed; I hadn't noticed clouds as I walked to the church that morning. It irritated me like a bad omen, a sentencing on Stephen's awful death that I must ignore. The lights flickered and the thunder blared. "No, I won't evade facts," I thought, "the weather is illustrating Stephen's life."

"The passing local cloud cover must never be mistaken for general darkness," Elder Maxwell began. "Stephen is going to have to work through whatever Heavenly Father wants him to work through...and Stephen will do it. He has taken with him all his fine qualities. They are not to be rescinded. They are to be further developed." Another flash of light diffused through the tall windows in the chapel and back through the cultural hall. "He will work his way through"—thunder roared—"without the chemical imbalance that afflicted him here. Finally, mercy overpowereth justice." The rumbling concluded with a boisterous swirl.

And weeks later a close friend said, "When the funeral commenced in that electrical storm, I knew Stephen had arrived in heaven."

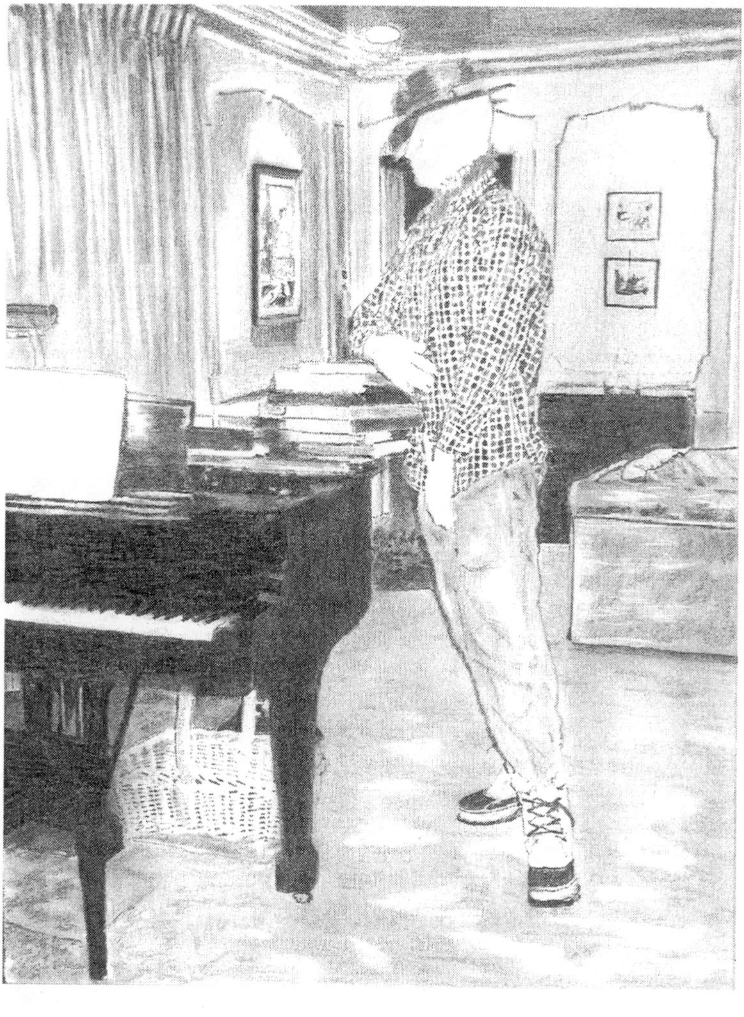

twenty-one

Angus

Down the sidewalk three-year-old John came leaping as bare as we had left him in the bathtub, holding a washcloth too small to cover what he knew was private. He kept repositioning it from side to side. Lloyd and I had been walking on the first warm day of spring. Six houses down the street we passed a neighbor chasing one of her children and calling to another to quit picking the geraniums.

"I'm so embarrassed," she said. She had caught the runaway and grabbed the flower picker with her other hand. "No problem for us," I laughed. "We've seen it all."

"You make us appreciate," Lloyd said, "how long it's been since we had the freedom to take a walk without worrying."

That's when we all turned around to hear John shouting, "Where are you going?"

John was born a joker. He disrupted class work with funnyman commentary. Each school year I prepared for the worst not knowing whether he would be disciplined or endured. His fourth grade teacher fathomed the value of humor.

"That is very funny, John," she said, over and over again. "But this is not the right time."

John was in her class when Stephen died. He did not laugh for days after. Neither did my other children.

The young man who had given them motorcycle rides years ago came over to cheer us up. "Remember when we bought that big innertube…we'd roll it out on the front lawn and bounce until someone would land on that metal valve that stuck out so far…Stephen and Mike smelled like grass clippings and gasoline…Barkley's slobber was mixed in there somewhere." My children sat listening; they were lightening up. Stephen had been dead three days. "Then we'd all wrestle on the lawn," he said. "I could get you guys in a pile and tickle you until Rebecca got mad or Mike threatened to wet his pants." Now they were smiling.

"And in the winter when we took the innertube sledding at the golf course, I remember Stephen had wiped out on a run and he was looking down at us from half way up the hill, just standing there when a guy on another tube knocked him flying. I thought he would really be hurt, but Stephen did a back flip in the air and landed on his feet!" I watched them all laugh. Good humor, that death had obscured, was returning.

Mike made a tape in the week following the funeral— journal entries of Stephen. It included things a parent might not want to know, intertwined with stories I wouldn't want to have missed. Mike commenced the recording sad and lonely. "I remember our talks…we were always talking…planning…I remember our goals…" The stories flowed.

"We were 12 or 13. We had planned to sleep on the patio," Mike said, "and then snuck out to visit neighbors down the street. They had tents set up in the backyard so we climbed in. A while later I heard my mother whispering, 'Stephen, Mike, are you in there?' We stayed quiet until she walked away. I felt guilty and decided to try and beat her home going another way. Stephen said he would follow. I ran around the block, climbed the neighbor's fence, did the Rambo maneuver across the grass in the moonlight and lunged onto my sleeping bag. Mom was lying next to me. 'Where's Stephen?' she said."

Mike made me laugh. He wasn't trying to. He hadn't planned to give me the tape but he knew I needed it. Everything I read in my journal to remember Stephen was serious.

"I recall the first basketball game Stephen refereed," Mike said. "The whistle blew and I knew Stephen had done it accidentally. I looked into his eyes and realized he would call one on me. 'Three seconds in the key' he shouted. Later in the game, during a time out, he asked the score keeper if he could call a foul that had already occurred.

"'How long ago?'

"'About five minutes,' Stephen said." Mike laughed onto the tape. Stephen had been laughing when he arrived home that night. "I didn't know what I was doing," he said. "They gave me a whistle—I had to use it for something."

There had been no point in making fun of Stephen since he had already laughed at himself. That was not easy for Stephen to do. For me it was even more difficult.

"I don't think I have a sense of humor," I told Liz. "I don't get most jokes."

"Don't worry, Mom," she said. "You create humor." Laughter is a gauge of my children's happiness. But when it's my mistakes, my fears they laugh about, I am slow to join in. I know that the most embarrassing blunders have the longest life expectancy.

We went to Mexico again a year after Stephen died. I

thought there was no reason for Andrew to miss the first two periods of school. We weren't leaving until 11:30 A.M. Andrew's bag was ready. My list was down to one load of wash, three errands and final packing. Andrew hesitated; walking to school he would be late. Together we ran to the Datsun parked aiming at the street—no backing up or turning around that morning. I switched on the key, many times, imagining the dead battery would revive and we could drive onto the street. Then in one movement I shifted into our van, revved the motor and pursued the path I had anticipated— crunching to a stop under the short side of the carport. I sat there, determined to solve the problem from inside the car. I told Andrew to get out and look.

"Do I back up or go forward?"

Andrew stood speechless. I jumped out by him and walked backwards, slowly, to comprehend the view. The double carport was leaning on the van. The cemented corner posts had popped out of the ground dismantling a forty foot "I" beam that smashed the windshield and bounced onto asphalt in the driveway. For twenty-one years we had lived with that carport. For fifteen of those years we owned a van too tall to clear the east side. Rush hour traffic to the University was moving slowly past our house. Hundreds of people had plenty of time to watch the spectacle. Lloyd returned home from work. "Should I cancel my trip?" I asked.

"No, you must go," he said. Today I wonder if his response was humorous but that day I thought it was pure charity.

Lloyd introduced me to humor. Our courtship was mostly by correspondence. He was in town for a last sorority dance before our marriage. "We don't have to go," I said. Lloyd was enthusiastic, cordial to my friends the whole evening. I don't remember what the intermission entertainment was but I do know Lloyd joked aloud during it. I am no judge but I guessed his wit would have been funny a few years earlier. I had already discerned that his tastes, developed in the 50s, didn't match mine of the 60s. But I also knew his peers laughed at each others' jokes and his brothers roared at ludicrous stories. Their favorite was about Grandfather Perkins who had lost a leg in a mining accident; he lived in Magna and worked at Kennecott Copper. He had bought a new suit and while his wife was away shopping, he proceeded to measure and cut off the extra pant leg. When Grandma returned he showed her the finished product proudly displaying it in front of him until he looked down to see; the wrong side was missing. I pitied the man I had never met until I realized he had probably told them the story himself. Laughter made Lloyd and his family feel so good that I knew they were sympathetic, not mean. I learned to trust their humor.

Many times since the sorority dance Lloyd has saved an otherwise boring evening for me by flavoring conversation with jokes. The ones I don't understand he explains to me privately and rarely repeats himself, as far as I know.

We had been married a decade before I learned humor was inheritable. As a child Cathy smiled all over her face. She learned from Lloyd to lift one side up and let the other down, switching her jaws back and forth and wiggling her ears. She was quiet and mischievous and adored by everyone. In school her teachers tried to pacify me over her mediocre performance. "She's just average. There's nothing wrong with that." But in her head she was laughing. Cathy perceived the world as a caricature of itself. Teachers were playing games. Conventional life was full of masks and everything she saw looked funny.

Christmas appealed to her like April Fools' Day. She played with Santa's presents all night, getting her fun out of acting surprised in the morning. She carried a squirt gun to Sunday School and hid it between her knees, shooting the teacher from under her dress. "If I got in trouble I was sick," Cathy told me when she was grown. "I didn't want people to say, 'Cathy, you know you shouldn't have.' I knew I shouldn't have and did it anyway."

I was beginning to understand Cathy when Mike evidenced the same outlook. The only difference was the noise level. Mike's jokes blasted for ten minutes. They crossed the ocean, trekked the outback, thrived in cages, delivered a high jumping kangaroo safely on the dock, and ended with the cry of "radio." The fact that nobody understood the nonsensical jokes left us all feeling uneasy and Mike fulfilled. I figured out, even as Mike sneezed dozens of times into his hands sporting green slime, that the only way to raise mature humor is to tolerate the developing kind.

Stephen made humor by incongruities. One week he pulled back the carpet and taped a four square on the floor. The next week he hit range balls in his room until he broke a window. He liked to surprise Mike by shooting arrows into the closet door, cutting his sheet with a machete and hurling himself like a flying eagle onto sleeping persons.

When I discovered the broken window, the battered door, and the machete missing from my Mexican treasures (the sheet disappeared) I was not amused. But my reaction was part of Stephen's entertainment. In that respect Cathy and Mike responded similarly. To them, a mischievous act became humorous when Mom was upset. Cathy and Mike secreted Hogan in the bathroom. "Mom walked in and yelled for about 20 minutes," Cathy wrote to Stephen in Hawaii. "Oh well, now Hogan is really clean."

I was not the sole recipient of their antics. Anyone caught in the line of sight was a target. Emily stayed away. She was safe the Saturday afternoon I trafficked garage sales with Stephen and Mike; she used the time preparing for her date. Hours before she had started with a shampoo and manicure, then the selection of clothes, the facial. We returned to a frenzy of activity that Emily was watching from the far side of the kitchen table dressed in pink. Liz was fixing dinner for a college group and Cathy was finishing a giant hoagie for the boy who invited her to the homecoming dance. Emily's date arrived in a tuxedo and was invited into the kitchen just as

Mike aimed at her face with a water pistol he claimed was empty. It rained on her forehead, over one eye, and onto her cheek. All activity froze while we waited for Emily's response. A clash was inevitable—it would not be a pretty sight in front of her date.

"Good thing I wear quality makeup," she said. "It's waterproof."

At that moment I knew Emily was mature enough to enjoy life. She married her date.

Pranks may not be a legitimate form of humor but they play effectively with tension. Rebecca, the most unlikely instigator, duped every one of us. She prepared a pitcher of chilled water, salt and red food coloring on a hot day in Tennessee which she served on the back porch.

Ten years later our family was vulnerable to acts of greater sophistication. Caught in the crossfire of a prank war amongst the older boys, Andrew was duct taped in place on the toilet. That act became the acknowledged extreme. Afterwards, the boys formed rules of their own—the prank must be something the victim activates—no putting tooth paste on sheets, but setting someone up to sit on an open tube was legitimate. Pranks supplied the leveling role of humor; no one in our family was allowed to live without distraction.

Lloyd fooled Stephen with the kind of humor they both liked best. The years Stephen lived away Lloyd wrote letters inconspicuously dated April 1. "We have been able to earn extra money by leasing your room to an oriental couple. They are quiet and self sufficient. Since they have no kitchen they have been using a hibachi in the window well. We stored your things [except for rugs and furniture] in the Christmas closet. Unfortunately that area flooded again last week but only the bottom boxes were damaged. The hesitation we had about this couple was their cat. Since you can't get hay fever long distance, we figured the clean-up would be pretty insignificant in comparison to the overall advantage."

Another year Lloyd wrote, "Two Sheriff Deputies came

to the front door and asked if we'd be interested in renting Hogan to the county for training in the K-9 Corps at $150.00 a month. We're not sure we want to do it…we don't have to decide until next week."

By the last year Lloyd was mixing in facts to offset the incredible. "We are still short on water in the mountains. No boats will be able to launch at Bear Lake this year. The Hot Spring facilities are being converted into a mud wrestling arena…"

Stephen would never say at what point he recognized the spoofs but he always acknowledged they were good for laughs. He elicited laughter by doing the absurd. He ate bugs attracted to the lantern at campouts instead of M & Ms. In stores he skateboarded, tipped shelves of videos, and answered telephones. Mike laughed around him constantly. So did Stephen's friends.

"How much should I pay for a mannequin?" he asked during fall quarter at the university. We reasoned together that the one for sale at a department store close-out was fairly priced.

"It still costs too much for a joke," he said. "Watch for a cheap one, Mom."

The next Friday I awakened in the night and wandered through the house. Everything looked normal. No lights left on meant everyone was in and usually that doors were double bolted. Brightness from the highway filtered through the curtains so I walked through the illuminated rooms first and then back down the dark hall. There were lots of dishes in the sink but the sideboards were cleared. I knocked into a stool sticking out from under the table and stumbled into the hall. I did not scream but I had to catch my balance on the railing. A mannequin dressed in a Levi jacket, bandanna and a cowboy hat stood in my way.

Stephen smiled at me the next morning. "Did you meet Angus?" he asked. For the next few days Angus met me all over the house in different outfits. I never adjusted. Encountering him standing by the piano in daylight scared me as much as finding him in front of the kitchen sink at night. Stephen took Angus with him to visit friends, to the convenience store. Stephen would stand him in line at the counter or set him up by the video machines until he was noticed. People asked to borrow him. The following weekend Angus was in an accident—he broke in half at the waist when he was run over by a jeep. Stephen and Mike taped him back together. Clothed, he looked no different but Stephen was upset.

"Angus does not leave this house without me!" he said. In reality, Stephen did not leave without Angus. Finally, Stephen carried him to a fraternity stomp and stood him by the refreshment table in a flannel shirt and jeans. People started laughing when Angus joined the dancing. Stephen laughed too. Several numbers later his hand was missing, then an arm, his head was smashed. People continued to slap each other on the back as they kicked Stephen's joke around the floor.

"Angus is dead," Stephen said later that night, punching at the kitchen cupboards with his fist.

"His knuckles were bleeding," Mike told me.

"It hurts!" he yelled. Then Stephen hit another cupboard door, angry at the pain. Martha cleaned up after him. Mike took him riding in the car so he wouldn't awaken us and get in trouble. That was one of the stories we didn't hear until long after it happened.

"Too much joking is sad, Mike," I said. "It can hurt—it can kill."

As quickly as I spoke I recognized that an absence of humor was just as dangerous. I rarely laughed for several months after Stephen died. Lincoln described "the fearful strain that was on me night and day. If I did not laugh I should die."

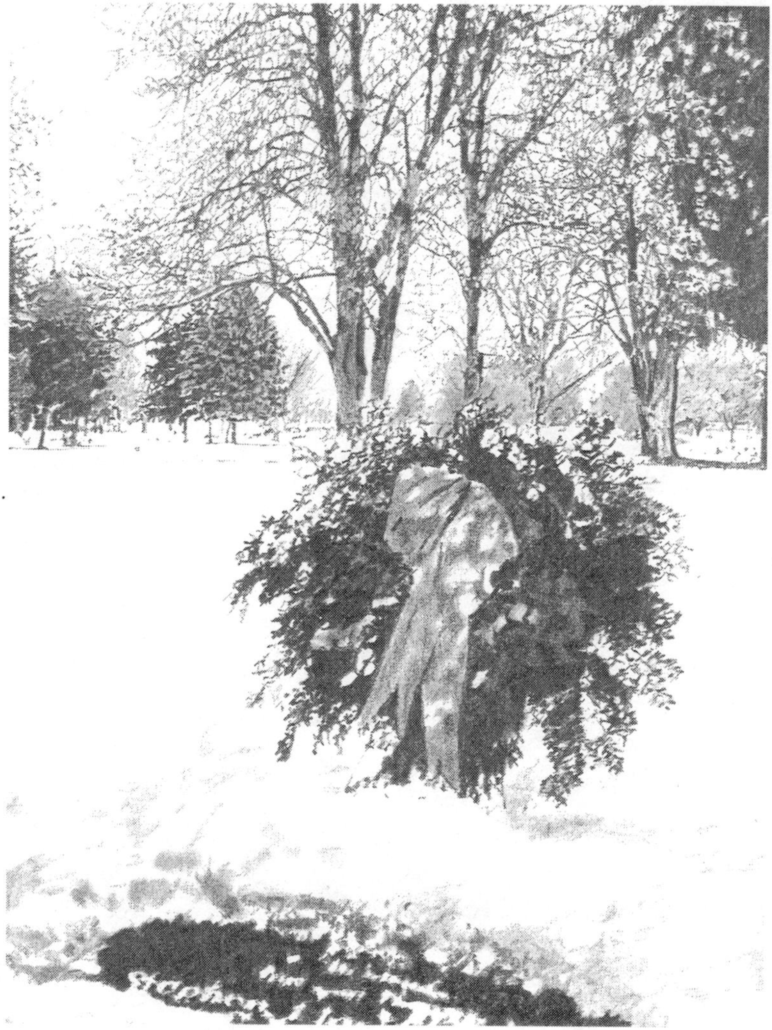

twenty-two

Cemeteries

"They're out of pain," a doctor said of his sleeping patients, and I think that of the dead.

"But what about evil people?" a student said. "Isn't that a broad generalization?" I can only respond with how I feel. I like going to cemeteries. While I'm there, I pause at graves with fresh flowers to look at dates, feeling a bond with strangers who put bouquets there. But most of all, I'm content.

In warm weather, I took my youngest children, a blanket, and stories to read by Stephen's grave. My mother was concerned. She had no desire to visit the cemetery where my father was buried. "You're not expecting to find Stephen there, are you?" she asked.

Weeks later, while I was spending the day with her, she fixed two plates of chicken salad garnished with parsley and a bottle of chilled juice. She suggested we go and eat by my father's grave. We sat under a pine tree looking at the mountains. Mother reminisced about the day she and father had bought their burial site. "Just look at the gorgeous view!" the saleswoman had said.

Stephen's first birthday after his death was painful. I awoke early Sunday morning and hurried into the utility room to dismantle a long garland I had brought home from a Christmas party the night before. Handel's *Messiah* played on the boom box while I wept, rearranging the evergreen boughs and wiring them into a wreath. I trimmed the streamers of red ribbon to scale. It didn't matter that I had forgotten to buy a wreath on Saturday. I knew Stephen would have preferred my frugal creativity. As soon as the children awoke, we left for the cemetery. I had pulled on Stephen's boots— with wool liners three sizes too big—over my slippers and I wore his jacket over my sweats.

"We look pretty awful," Martha said as we drove. Great, I thought. We aren't in sackcloth, but close enough. I set the wreath on the snow. It lay flat and insignificant. Then we noticed other wreaths supported on wire stands; the children gathered sticks to prop it up. I stood firmly in the snow, wishing to languish in that place as long as possible. It was easy to relive the past.

"Choose your favorite food," I had told Stephen weeks before his twelfth birthday. For birthday treats, I knew without asking that Liz would love her own case of bananas, Rebecca home canned pickled beets, Emily dill pickles, and Cathy extra cream cheese icing on a carrot cake. Stephen had sat next to me at the table with a whole cherry cheese cake in front of him, too excited to eat a bite. "Mom, save it for me! I'll eat it all, later."

The children had forgotten to bring gloves to the cemetery. They had the wreath braced and were blowing on their fingers.

Two years ago on December 8 I had gone shopping with Stephen for his birthday presents. I had wanted to buy him a cure. "I think it's the cold that drives you away in the winter," I said to Stephen. "Choose something you'll wear." Instead of shopping at the usual bargain places, I surprised us both by walking into the mall and paying full price for a green and white Nautica jacket and wool gloves. Stephen wore them to the university, to work, to movies and to "decorate" the Newman's yard down the street. "It looks great, Mom. They're living in a forest!" Stephen and Mike had collected fifty discarded trees after Christmas and stood them around the neighbor's house in the snow. Cathy helped them paint a huge banner, "USED CHRISTMAS TREES FOR SALE," which they hung in front of the house and decorated with miniature lights.

We walked back to the car. Lloyd came home for lunch. "Great wreath!" he said. "I could see it from the car." My vision blurred. Lloyd had triggered more emotion that continued in me for the rest of the day, embarrassing everyone I saw.

I went to bed reading *A Christmas Carol*. "I will live in the Past, the Present and the Future," Scrooge said. "I will not shut out the lessons that they teach."

They promised to install Stephen's grave stone; it had been almost a year and I was finally in a hurry. I had been to the cemetery two days in a row hoping they might be working. It was nearly the last thing I could do for Stephen. Most of his possessions had been distributed. We all wore his clothes, feeling closer to him that way. Lloyd and the other children used the keyboard.

Months earlier Lloyd had asked me if I would write about Stephen's life. I answered promptly, "Never. It's too complicated." But I could not help it. As I walked I remembered the winter day sitting at my desk, when I had an impression like

C.S. Lewis described, when Stephen's mind momentarily faced my own. I had been working for days on the chapter about the stone fort, rereading Stephen's journals and mine. Nothing I had written fit together. I was doubting my ability to communicate his story accurately. I wanted to tell the truth without "froth or tinsel."

"So be it," I could have said as Lewis did, "Look your hardest, [Stephen]. I wouldn't hide if I could. We didn't idealize each other…You knew most of the rotten places in me already. If you now see anything worse, I can take it. So can you."

Then the chapter fell into place; the order of events had been wrong before. I pounded my desk and asked aloud, who is helping me? Is it you, Stephen?

Again Lewis said, "I had never in any mood imagined the dead as being so—well, so business-like. Yet there was an extreme and cheerful intimacy. An intimacy that had not passed through the senses or emotions at all…

"Wherever it came from, it has made a sort of spring cleaning in my mind…Brisk? cheerful? keen? alert? intense? wide-awake? Above all, solid. Utterly reliable. Firm. There is no nonsense about the dead."

When the gravestone was in place I returned to the cemetery with my mother and Liz, both visiting from out of town. We had put violets in the vase holder when my mother's neighbor discovered us; the coincidence was surprising. She had been standing by a grave nearby and walked over to look at the marker, "Oh, he was so young, how did he die?"

Here we go again, I thought. I have been dealing with this for a year. I'll feel better if I am completely honest. It may be painful to others but I'll risk it.

"He took his own life," I said. Now the lady was miserable; she couldn't speak. She hadn't wanted to cause pain. I couldn't leave her suffering.

"He was not well, chemically," I added. The woman clung to the explanation.

"Oh...yes...I understand. I have a grandchild who is on medication..." The lady left and we stood quietly.

Something was wrong. I had hurt that woman. She was innocent and I made her feel guilty. I had forged ahead with my answer; the sensation was familiar. That's what I did when I got on a motorcycle, when I rescued the Laotian's masks, but this time the result was not favorable.

Liz stood by my mother; they were both in agony. Living away they didn't face frequent reminders from people about Stephen.

"Do you get asked questions like that a lot?"

"No, never before."

"Wouldn't it be better to explain first that Stephen had been ill?"

I tried to think if that would be cowardly. Would I be shielding myself from accepting the blame for my share of Stephen's problems? I still carried my own burden. If I had given him more love, more praise, maybe I could have prolonged his life.

The next week I sat across the desk from my doctor for an annual check-up. He paused, put the chart to one side, and said, "I've been thinking about you. I have an eighteen-year-old son. At age fourteen he started making bad choices. He went with the wrong group and now I don't see him changing. You are a responsible parent. Tell me you don't feel guilty about your son."

"I feel sad."

"I understand. But you don't feel guilty do you? I have done everything I can for my son. I have given him opportunities. I have encouraged him. But he rejected it. Now I work to accept my son and love him the way he is. I don't feel guilty. I hope you don't."

My doctor was as sad as I was. He hadn't quit being a parent, though he felt he was having about as much impact on his son as I currently did on Stephen. We had both arrived at a new phase of love.

I am almost finished writing. I had ended once before when spring had come and gone again. Andrew and John went with me in the summer to study Spanish in Mexico, traveling on buses and trains for days all the way to Cuernavaca. It was Friday of my first week of classes; a different agenda allowed an hour of singing with Gabriella and two hundred students packed into Sala C. She sat on a stool in her embroidered poncho next to a microphone, her dulcet voice carrying us through the songbook—*Eres Tu, Des Colores*, then *Cielito Lindo*, the familiar one—I didn't need to read the words. "*Ay Ay Ay Ay, canta no llores*," yes, "sing don't cry," I translated in my mind, "*Porque cantando se alegran...*" a wave of grief washed over me. I could see Stephen lying dead in the hospital, in the mortuary, in the church. I could see the closed coffin in the cemetery. I could not stop the tears I had learned to make. I hid my face with the songbook. They sang on, the chorus repeated after all three verses. I shifted out of Gabriella's line of vision. I could not stop, not even with the end of the song. Stephen's dead! Surrounded by hundreds in the city of eternal spring, I froze, stuck on death. I could not get him up, out of the coffin.

"Help me, O Lord, to comprehend the living Stephen."

Ten minutes later, it was over. I was restored. I knew I would see Stephen again in a future place.

"I think I'll buy burial plots," Lloyd said twenty-five years ago when we were young parents. We had stood together on the section of the cemetery named Cypress Hill.

"It's no priority for me," I told him.

"They're available. We'd probably never get a location as nice when we need it."

I looked across the rolling lawn to trees that skirted Mount Olympus. We trimmed around the stone of his father's grave and arranged the iris in a juice can on the grass. Lloyd sang

Scottish songs, like his father. They were Harry Lauder favorites—*Just A Wee Deoch-An-Doris, Breakfast In Your Bed on Sunday Marnin'*. Liz, age 3, had twirled in circles holding a small American flag in her hand. Rebecca toddled after her.

"My parents will laugh," I said, "if we purchase a burial site now."

"Your parents will probably need one before my brothers and sisters and none of my family have any interest either. Sometimes I think," he said, "what if we had a child die..."

I imagined a little coffin, so foreign next to our lively children around us. I wasn't unhappy with Lloyd for introducing the subject. This was a practical matter—four family plots needed to be sold to meet his mother's expenses. But the notion annoyed me. I had been similarly irritated on our wedding day. I was dressed in white, ready to kneel at the altar, when the officiator had intruded on my bliss. The words I dreaded he would say cut beyond the celebration. I had resisted his experienced perspective.

"Life will get difficult..."

Stop, I thought. Don't tell me that, even if it's true.

"As you go through adversity you will learn..."

This is gloomy—it's diluting my joy. I had stashed the realities in the back of my mind. As we sat in the cemetery with our first young children, I repressed the possibility of a child's coffin too. I was determined to enjoy the present!

But what if the present becomes tragic? My mind had dared ask a question I was too scared and inexperienced to examine.

"Go ahead, Lloyd," I said. "Buy the plots."